MW01296908

Inside the Mirror Box

Spells and Theory for All Practitioners

Ray Baker

2015
Independently Published
Wichita, Kansas U.S.A.

First Edition 2015

Library of Congress Cataloging Data Pending

ISBN-13: 978-1514882351
ISBN-10: 1514882353

Written in Wichita, Kansas. Proudly published independently through Amazon.com, Inc. using CreateSpace.

Special Thanks:

To Natalie Phi-Halstead, Michael "Ethan" Salcedo, Amanda Lind, Janiece Baum Dixon, Jennifer Dominick, and Jola Daniels for taking the time to copy edit and give feedback. Also to my friends and family for listening to me carry on and on about this book for two long years.

A VERY special thank you to everyone who inspired the spells in these pages through your actions, both good and bad. I couldn't have done it without you!

Disclaimers:

The information in this book is for educational purposes only, and is not intended to replace the care or advice of a medical doctor, lawyer, psychiatrist, or other licensed professional. The author takes no responsibility for the decisions of the reader in regards to how the information contained herein is used.

All efforts have been made to ensure that no one can be identified by the anecdotes in this book. The names of those involved have been omitted, and in many cases their genders or relationships between one another changed in the strongest attempt possible to protect their identities.

Table of Contents

Introduction
The Hall of Mirrors

Imagine yourself standing before a large, square mirror. You stare pensively into your own eyes as you reflect on all your life experiences, and everything you've done and become. You reach out to touch the tips of your fingers to the glass. The person in the mirror does the same. You crack a half smile, knowing that you're face to face with yourself like you've never been before. The mirror shows your every perfection, every flaw, and every intricacy of your being. You gaze at your reflection as your thoughts wander through the adventure known as your life.

After a long moment, you come back to the present. You turn to walk away. But instead of walking into a hallway or room, you find yourself staring at your reflection again. You spin around. Giant mirrors surround you. You look toward the sky, only to see yourself staring back down from above. Your gaze drops frantically to the floor, hoping to find solid ground. Instead, your face looks up at you from an endless string of reflections inside reflections inside reflections. You spin in circles, trying to find a way out. The reflections dance about as each mirror duplicates your image hundreds of times over in the others. You become lost in the swirling images that bounce back at you from every direction. You lose track of left and right; up and down, all while your own reflection closes in on you.

Finally, you collapse. You bury your face in your knees, and close your eyes tightly, unable to face what you see in the images that surround you. You know that if you open your eyes, you'll be lost again in the dark storm of reflections crashing down on you. So you sit quietly with your eyes closed, and hope for darkness — the only thing that will make the mirrors go black.

You've found your way inside the mirror box. In this giant hall of mirrors, your true self stares back at you from every direction. Your actions — both good and bad — are amplified a hundred times over, and sent back to you with no holding back. There's no way to escape once you're trapped inside. All you can do is sit back, and own up to what you've sent into the world as it shines back on you with the brutal honesty that only the mirrors can declare. The mirrors will decide when the ride is over.

While this illustration is obviously exaggerated, it describes the spiritual effects of one of the most well-known and effective spells used by practitioners of many magickal paths. Mirror spells can be found in Voodoo, Hoodoo, Pow-wow, Wicca, and many other systems that have strong roots in folk magick. Their powerful symbolism and fast action have made mirrors a staple in magickal supply cabinets, as well as a popular find in many spell books. Some mirror spells focus on looks, where the practitioner transforms a mirror into a beauty altar to glamour themselves into being more confident or attractive. Others involve sending back negativity by burning a candle upside down over a mirror. Some mirrors are painted black and used as divination tools to see into the future, or gain unknown information. My favorite mirror spell, however, is the mirror box, which surrounds the target from every direction with the intent of reflecting certain energies toward or away from them.

As you saw in the illustration, the most popular use of the mirror box is for returning negative energies to their sender. A basic version of this spell involves constructing a box of mirrors that all face inward. A picture of the person causing problems, a personal effect, or their name written on a slip of paper is then added before sealing on the lid. It's said that the energies they send out are blocked on all sides, then immediately sent back with more force than what was first sent out. You might believe this law of return to be threefold, sevenfold, tenfold, or more, depending on your magickal background. What matters most is that the energies are sent back to the person with extra force, which will push them to stop their negative behavior, and put them back in line.

The second most popular use of the box is as a protection spell to guard the target from unwanted people or influences. In this case, the box is constructed with all of the mirrors facing outward before the personal effect or target's name is sealed inside. This creates a magickal force field around the individual that reflects back any negativity that comes their way. In this way, the box can be used to protect someone from an abusive partner, gossipy co-workers, a handsy boss, or even bad luck in general.

Most practitioners learn only these two uses for the mirror box. While these are perfect examples of its power, I've come to discover in my workings that it can be much more versatile. I've definitely used it for return to sender spells, warding, and protection. However, it's also great for bringing the truth to light, helping one face their fears, making yourself a more likeable person, and attracting success and prosperity. I've even put myself in the mirror box to help me through several difficult situations. With a little creativity, the possibilities of the mirror box are limitless — which is exactly why it has become one of the most important pieces of my magickal toolset.

Learning First Hand

I first heard about the mirror box at a gathering in my hometown. I was in my early twenties, and had been attending monthly full moon circles held by the local Pagan community. While mingling after one of the circles, I was eavesdropping on a conversation between another young witch and one of the elders. The younger witch explained that her husband was abusing her on a regular basis. She wasn't satisfied with the way the police were handling the situation, so she wanted to try a spell that would permanently remove him from her life. She asked the elder for a strong working that would both make her soon-to-be ex pay for the abuse he'd caused her and her two children, and also banish him from their lives for good.

I listened in as the elder explained how to construct a box of mirrors that all faced inward, and that placing the man inside the box would make all of the trouble he caused reflect back on him. Eventually, she continued, things would get so bad for him that he would be driven out of their lives altogether — either by finally landing in jail, or by getting so caught up in his own evil that it would drive him away. She also explained that the young woman should put herself in a box of mirrors that faced outward to protect herself from further harm he might try to cause.

I've always been a fan of highly figurative spells, so I found the symbolism behind the device brilliant. In my own spells, I always try to pick correspondences and symbols that will almost exactly act out what I want to happen. The mirror box struck me as a spell that I could really get into, since I would be able to see the results play out in my mind as I did the working. I jotted down the elder's instructions when I got home, and added them to my book of shadows.

A few weeks later, as if the spell had come to me for a reason, I got a chance to test drive it when I started having problems with a manager at work. I was working as an animal caretaker for a local museum that was having serious financial problems. This particular manager was anxious to make cuts, and had been trying to dissolve my position for some time. Thankfully for me, the boss above him saw that I was a hard worker, and that my job was an important part of the museum. Therefore, he refused to buckle under the pressure being put on him to let me go.

Or so I thought, until I received a minor injury on the job. I was kneeling down in the aquarium room spraying out a water dish with a hose that was connected to a utility sink. The hose had knocked a heavily taped cord for one of the aquarium lights out of place, and caused it to land on the metal faucet. Not realizing that the wire was touching the faucet, I reached up to shut off the water after rinsing out the dish. With the wet hose in one hand, and the metal knob in the other, I got to witness firsthand the powerful magick known as electricity.

Luckily, the aquarium light was plugged into a GFCI circuit breaker (commonly found in bathrooms where electrical devices are used over sinks and tubs), which cut my cook time short. After assessing the damage (a small electrical burn on my hand, a little fuzziness in my head, and a fried aquarium light with a bad cord) I decided that there was no real harm done. I shook it off, and went on about my day.

My mistake was that — in trying to laugh it off — I had told several coworkers about the incident right after it happened. The next day, word had gotten back to the director of the museum that I had been "electrocuted" in the aquarium room, and had failed to report the incident. I was reprimanded for not filling out a formal accident report, and suspended from my Animal Care duties for one month. I was then moved to a lower position doing school group intake, and cleaning up after the hundreds of tiny tornadoes that ripped through the various pavilions each day.

Despite the fact that I disagreed with the director's decision, I decided to lay low, and ride out the suspension period. But my manager had already sank his teeth into the opportunity to not only fire me, but to try to eliminate my department altogether. I was called back into the director's office a few days into my suspension. The director slid a sheet of paper across his desk. He asked me to read it, and explain to him what it said. As my eyes scanned the page, I read a one-page report of what had happened in the aquarium room a few days before. The entire thing was written from the point of view of my manager — who wasn't even there during the incident — and not only exaggerated the event, but flat-out lied about it.

I tried to explain to the director what had actually happened, and that the manager who wrote the report wasn't in the room when I was shocked. Nor had he attempted to interview me personally about the incident. The director agreed to look into it before deciding what action he should take, then sent me back to work.

As I tend to do in situations like this, I immediately went to my spell book when I got home. Getting me suspended from my position wasn't enough. My manager wasn't going to stop until he had my job. I slammed my book open. My first instinct was to look up one of my faithful threefold spells. Instead, I found the instructions for the mirror box — which I had scrawled on a pink post-it note — stuck right inside the cover. Even better, I just happened to have a pack of frameless compact mirrors stashed in my closet, which I had been saving for an art project that I never got around to. The spell was begging me to give it a try.

The working itself was a piece of cake. I taped the mirrors together, leaving the top open so I could throw in a slip of paper with my manager's name. I also wrote a short description of the trouble he was causing, and sprinkled in a few herbs for protection and returning negativity to its sender. After reciting a chant I wrote to fit the working, I sealed the lid on with wax from a black candle I had been burning during the spell. When I was done, I left the box in the center of my altar so I could shake it while repeating the chant whenever I felt the need.

By the time I got to work the next day the director had interviewed several coworkers. Everyone he spoke to had come to my defense. The best part was that several of our on-site handy men had also come forward to deem many of the claims in my manager's falsified report as impossible. The maintenance manager refused to sign the report, and shot down many of the lies my manager tried to get over on the museum's director. The glamour he had over upper management was shattered, and his true motives revealed. Not only was he asked to turn in his resignation, but I was removed from suspension, and the incident was completely forgotten about.

I was so amazed at how well the box worked that I started turning to it more and more often. Soon, I was integrating it into other kinds of spells to see if it could lend the same speed and power to workings other than protection and warding. Sure enough, with a little creativity, the right correspondences, and a well-written chant, I was able to use it for just about anything. Through experimentation and ingenuity, I've compiled a network of spells based on the mirror box that has blossomed over time into its own system of magick. My spell book is now full of various workings that employ the mirror box. All of which originate from the basic banishing and protection spells that I learned during the gathering more than a decade ago.

Now, like the elder I first learned it from, the mirror box is the first thing I suggest when a friend is in need of strong, fast-acting magick. Most recently, I shared the spell with a friend who was having trouble with an obsessive ex. What started as a few too many text messages had quickly turned into breaking into his apartment while he was at work, stealing from his home, and attempted blackmail. He needed something that would put a quick stop to the craziness, and get his ex out of his life for good. The results blew him away to the point that we now have a running joke: any time one of us says or does something that goes a little too far, all we have to do is say *"espejos"* (Spanish for "mirrors") to let the other one know he has overstepped his bounds.

When I saw how well the box worked for my friend, I began to look back on the spells I had written. Doing so made me realize how much experience I've gained with it since casting that first spell on my manager. I became inspired to write this book once I saw the extent to which I was able to expand on this simple magickal tool. I wanted to show other witches just how flexible and powerful the mirror box can be. It's simple, inexpensive, extremely effective, and something that I feel every witch should master as part of their training. It's an invaluable addition to any magickal supply cabinet, not to mention a page in your book of shadows that you'll turn to over and over again. I'm convinced that once you read this book, you'll always keep a pack of mirrors on hand to help you through the toughest situations.

In the following chapters, I'll explain everything from where to get supplies to make the box, how to put it together, what to put in it, and the different ways to use it. I'll also give instructions on how to break spells and dispose of boxes once a spell has run its course. Of course, I'll provide you with all of the spells that I've performed with the mirror box to date. These are all spells that I've written myself, and are either based on the two main uses of the box, or were created by expanding on the general idea behind the original spells.

In many cases, I've written the events that inspired certain spells, and the results that I experienced *as I perceived them*. I especially want to stress that I've written everything from my own point of view. The outcomes of the spells are all based on *how I interpreted* the events that followed casting them. Could outside forces have played a large part in how things turned out in each case? Of course. Might some of the results I saw have happened anyway as part of the natural cause and effect of my targets' actions? I believe so. Could my spells have put many of those outside forces into action, and helped the events come about faster than they otherwise would have? In my opinion, and from my own point of view, absolutely.

Furthermore, I've kept the events themselves true to life as seen from my vantage point. The facts are all intact. I have, however, eliminated the real names of the people involved. I've changed most relationships between people (friends, relatives, exes, ex friends, exes of friends, ex friends of friends, exes of exes, et cetera) in order to protect the identities of those involved. One thing I don't want to do with this book is call out people from my past or present. It's not my intention to spread gossip or cause embarrassment, nor is it my right or responsibility. Furthermore, the vast majority of my readers would have no idea who I was talking about, and, therefore, wouldn't relate any better to the stories for knowing the original names or interpersonal relationships. My only intention is to educate other witches about mirror box magick using my personal experiences as my curriculum.

There will inevitably be those few people who read this, and think they recognize themselves by one of the stories in the book. Despite my tedious attempts to cover up names and relationships, some people might still try to fit themselves into one of my anecdotes based on the events that I discuss. To those people, I have just one thing to say: if you didn't want me to write bad things about you, you should've behaved better in the first place. Every now and then you mistreat the wrong person. Sometimes that person is a writer, and uses what you did as inspiration for a book that the entire world might see. Other times that person also happens to be a witch. Then, not only do they cast spells on you to throw back the ill will you sent their way, but they sometimes write a book about it later, too. ALWAYS think before you act. You never know how things might come back to haunt you.

Another thing I would like to point out is that this book doesn't include circle castings, quarter calls or other "witchcraft 101" instructional material. I've written this book for more advanced practitioners: those witches who already have a strong background in magick, and don't need to have their hand held along the way. Many practicing witches already have their own way of casting circles, calling quarters, opening their chakras, and so on (and some magickal paths don't perform these actions at all, even though they do cast spells, and perform other types of magick). I don't feel it necessary to repeat information that can be found in hundreds of other titles that deal with witchcraft, and how to become a practicing witch. My book doesn't focus on how to become a witch, but rather how to use what you already know to become more adept at a specific magickal tool that many traditions have come to use in their practice.

If you happen to be a beginner, then this book is probably not for you (at least not yet). I advise newcomers to keep this book in a safe place until they've done more research, and have gained more experience with magick. Mirror spells can be unpredictable. The energies that you sometimes have to work with can even be dangerous. The spells in this book should only be performed by those who have experience with how witchcraft works, and know what to expect during the manifestation of certain workings.

You'll also find that the majority of the spells in this book don't contain names of gods or goddesses. The main reason for this is that I don't believe in God. I believe that the different gods and goddesses throughout the world's religions are simply personifications of different natural forces and energies that the practitioner attempts to access during a working. For example, when I cast a spell to bring more love into my life, I don't believe that Aphrodite herself comes down from the sky, waves her hands over my altar, and makes my spell come true. I see Aphrodite as a name for the actual energy of love. She serves as an image that solidifies the abstract concept of love my mind. Where some practitioners might need to call on her — or another deity that represents love to them — in order to get in touch with that energy, I simply meditate on the energy itself to tap into its power.

Another reason I eliminated the spirits' names is that I want the spells to fit into the system you already have in place. People of many different magickal traditions can benefit from the power of the mirror box. Voodoo practitioners, Wiccans, old school Pagans, and shamans alike can all use it with great success. There are even Christians and Catholics who incorporate magick into their belief systems. Then there are those, like me, who are Atheists as far as their belief in God, but still use magick to get in touch with the natural energies that we share with the world around us. However you do your own thing, I want the spells in this book to work for you. Therefore, I've excluded certain elements that might point to a specific tradition to allow users to seamlessly blend their own practice into each working.

In the few cases that I do use a spirit's name in a working, there is usually a good reason. For one, it might fit the general theme of the spell. Themed spells unify the different elements in the working, and keep everything cohesive. They evoke strong images in the mind of the spell caster, which keeps their intent focused while performing the working. Sometimes the image of a spirit will be so strong that it immediately allows the practitioner to raise energy toward the spell. Other times, the very name of a deity instantly aligns the spell caster with the energy they want to connect with. In these cases, I've left the name and image in to assist in the casting of particular spells.

Other times, I'm simply fond of a certain spirit (their mythology or what they represent strikes a chord with me that helps me get in touch with that frequency of energy). While I might not believe they exist as a conscious being, I do believe that what they stand for can lend a tremendous amount of power to my working. But, again, this is purely out of the desire to sync myself with the specific energy they represent, and not out of worship or devotion, or even out of a vague belief in that particular entity.

At this point you, like many witches I've talked to, might be wondering how my spells work if there is no god or goddess overseeing them. I've encountered many people who believe wholeheartedly that the gods they call on are actual beings who manifest their spells. In reality, magick is simply interplay between different energies that occur in nature, and different levels of cause and effect. The practitioner uses various mental, physical, and spiritual actions to tap into these energies, then uses the force of their will to set a desired cause into action. This cause then creates an equal or opposite reaction, which is said to manifest the effect of the spell. The theory behind the process, as I'll show in the following pages, is actually based more on natural reciprocal laws than it is on supernatural powers.

How Mirror Boxes Work:
The Laws of Similarity and Contagion

Before diving into any magickal working, one should always understand exactly what they're dealing with, and how it works. Mirror boxes provide the perfect example of how and why magick functions the way it does. I'll cover the rules of mirror magick in chapter two, which are the guidelines for using magick ethically, and with the most productive results. For now, however, I want to explain the basic magickal theory behind spell casting as it relates to the mirror box.

The foundation of all magickal workings is laid down by the two most primitive — yet essential — magickal laws: The Law of Similarity and The Law of Contagion. These two laws govern every spell either separately or in conjunction with one another. Understanding how they work will not only help you grasp the functioning of the mirror box, but will also help you understand the theory on which all other magick is based. Once you understand Similarity and Contagion, you'll be able to better visualize exactly what happens when you cast spells, which will add that much more power to your workings.

While the Laws of Similarity and Contagion have been the force behind magick since the first spell was cast, it's said that they were first clearly defined in the book *The Golden Bough*, written by James George Frazer in 1890. In his work, Frazer defines the two laws as follows:

> Analysis shows that magic rests everywhere on two fundamental principles: first, that *like produces like*, effect resembling cause; second, that *things which have once been in contact continue ever afterwards to act on each other*. The former principle may be called the Law of Similarity; the latter, that of Contact or Contagion (7).

This short paragraph packs a lot of punch. At its core, it states that similar items or actions naturally attract one another. Many witches think of this as different things vibrating at similar frequencies of energy, which makes them attract those same energies when put to use in magick. We see this law at work when we choose correspondences for spells. Many witches associate the color red with love and passion, and therefore things that are red (such as roses, rubies, red hearts, etc) also come to be associated with love and passion. As will be discussed later, many ancient herbal remedies were classified in much the same way. For example, plants that were the same color or shape as certain body parts were oftentimes said to heal that body part when used as medicine.

Frazer goes on to explain that the Law of Similarity also states that a desired outcome can be obtained from a magickal working by acting it out during said working. This tells us that the actions we perform while casting a spell can have a direct effect on how the spell comes to fruition. While casting, we want to try to act out exactly what we want to happen as if we were performing a play that will come to life based on every word and action taken during the dress rehearsal. Therefore, the symbolism used in any spell holds a great deal of importance. We want to choose words, correspondences, and actions that mimic the results we want to achieve so that the energy we put out knows exactly what job it's supposed to do, and where to go to get it done.

Mirror spells are a prime example. For a return to sender spell, the practitioner symbolically places the target inside the box using some sort of personal effect. They then imagine that the mirrors are reflecting said target's negativity back on them, therefore making them reap the consequences of their actions. As the spell is performed, the physical props work together with the spoken words and spiritual energy to write a kind of script of events that the practitioner wants to manifest. In magickal theory, this script will be acted out as the spell comes to fruition.

Finally, the Law of Similarity reminds us that for every action there is an equal or opposite reaction. Like Newton's third law of motion, which is where the phrase originates from, the world tends to give back to us what we put in. When we perform any action — especially when we cast spells — we're creating a ripple (a cause) that we send out with a specific task (an effect) to perform. This is the basis of the Law of Return, which is what many people — witches or not — live by in one form or another. "Do unto others as you would have them do unto you," "what goes around, comes around," "you reap what you sow," and other adages all reflect the same idea. We're urged to treat others how we want to be treated, for we know that what we put into the world is what we ultimately get in return. This takes on an even deeper meaning in return to sender spells, where we cause a ripple that we hope will bring the effects of a negative person back home to make them pay — and hopefully learn from — the harm they've caused.

The second law, the Law of Contagion, is based on a personal link to the target of a spell. This usually involves a part of the person's body (hair, nail clippings, or even bodily fluids such as urine), or a personal effect of the target (anything they own, especially something they might miss such as a favorite trinket or shirt). The idea is that everything we touch in our daily lives becomes forever connected to us on an astral level. The closer the object is to the target on either a physical or sentimental level, the stronger the contagious bond will be.

Through the Law of Contagion, we can use the target's personal effect as a stand-in for their presence. Then, following the Law of Similarity, whatever is done to the stand-in will travel through that spiritual bond, like electricity through a power line, and will also be done to the target. Voodoo dolls work on the same principle, as do some mojo bags and witch jars, in which someone might be placed as the target of various operations. Mirror boxes work on the same magickal theory by symbolically placing the target inside so the energies that reflect back on or away from the personal effect are equally reflected on or away from the target.

If you break down any spell, you can see the Law of Similarity and the Law of Contagion at work in one form or another. Think back on some of the spells you have performed in the past. How were these two laws at work in some of your own workings? What items have you used as a personal effect? How did the results play out in comparison with what was said and done during the spell? Keeping these things in mind will help you understand how your spells are working, and why they turn out the way they do. You'll be better able to predict their outcomes, and also foresee any possible backlash or pitfalls that you might encounter along the way.

Furthermore, these two fundamental laws govern many other theories and rules of conduct throughout various magickal traditions. From this foundation, we learn that everything we do comes back to us to some degree. We learn that doing harm to others is essentially doing harm to ourselves. We learn that once we have touched someone, be it physically, mentally, or emotionally; be it to harm or to heal, we can never untouch them. Therefore, we learn the importance of using magick responsibly and appropriately — lest we destroy ourselves in the process.

A Look Into Another Dimension

As I was doing research for this book, I stumbled upon a blog run by photographer and author Ron Brinkmann. Brinkmann's blog, titled "Digital Composting," explores different topics and techniques in the world of photography and visual effects. The post that caught my attention was a photography experiment that Brinkmann performed with a box made of inverted mirrored tiles exactly like the ones used in the spells in this book. In the experiment, he sealed a small digital camera inside the box with various objects, set the timer, and snapped some amazing photos of what it looks like from inside the mirror box.

Although the blog itself isn't related to the magickal uses of the mirror box, the photos allow the viewer to step into the hidden dimension within its walls. From the outside, it seems like an ordinary box. Inside, however, it opens up into an infinite universe that surrounds and engulfs whatever gets trapped inside. I used the same process in a 12" x 12" inverted mirror box to create the photograph for the cover of this book. Like Brinkmann's photos, the cover photograph shows how anything inside the mirror box immediately gets lost in the endless string of repeated reflections as they spread out into infinity.

These photos are also a brilliant representation of the magickal theory on which the box is said to work. The pictures solidify the ideas behind the Laws of Similarity and Contagion as they relate to mirror magick by visually demonstrating the symbolism that the practitioner has in mind when they cast spells with the box. Just as the reflections are duplicated and reflected back on the target's personal effect in a never-ending string, so, too, are the actions of the spell's target infinitely augmented and reflected back on them for the duration of the working.

Furthermore, the photos show viewers the mirror box's connection with the astral plane, and why so many practitioners consider mirrors to be gateways to this realm. The mirror box acts as a portal between the physical world and the astral realm of the mind. On the physical plane, the inverted box is nothing more than a small glass cube. But once it's sealed, it bursts open into its own micro universe. It's in this alternate universe that the real magick is said to happen. The mirror box is simply the tool that connects that world to our own, and which activates the changes in the other dimension so that they can take place on the physical plane.

Due to printing restrictions, I was not able to include Brinkmann's original photographs in my book. To see the full color photos from his experiment, and to enjoy even more of his brilliant work, visit his blog "Digital Composting" at http://www.digitalcomposting.wordpress.com.

Ethics and Rules of the Mirror Box

White Magick or Black Magick?

Like the elder I first learned it from, I almost always bring up the mirror box when someone asks me to recommend a powerful spell. However, I've found that many witches — especially Wiccans — shy away from the topic once I start explaining different things that I've used the box for, and some of the results that I've seen. One question that always pops up is, "doesn't that constitute black magick?" Most people argue two perfectly legitimate concerns: that some of the spells seem to be designed to overtly harm others, and that by harming others those spells might backfire on the practitioner.

It's true that when using the mirror box on difficult people, the practitioner can walk a fine line between so-called "good" magick and "bad" magick. It's important to understand, however, that very few things in human nature are black and white, and nothing in nature is inherently good or evil. Magick is no exception. Just as a person's actions make them good or evil in the eyes of others, the way a practitioner uses the energies that they call up is what determines whether their working falls more toward the assumed "light side" or the "dark side".

In my experience, those who have opposed the mirror box are usually people who have been programmed to perceive the darker side of their talents as black magick. They've been taught that those energies can only be destructive, and sometimes even misled to believe that performing darker workings lies outside of their own understanding or abilities. Programming of this sort brings the practitioner's personal development to a screeching, tire-smoking halt that denies them access to an entire half of their abilities. Like yin without the yang, a witch who only uses the light side of their talents will be incomplete and imbalanced. Knowing when to use your darker abilities is the key, and is what defines the line between true black magick and performing acts of magickal self-defense. The distinction between the two is not only a moral issue, but also determines whether or not a working backfires on the practitioner.

It's commonly accepted that magick should never be used to impose on another person's freewill or opportunity to succeed, nor should it be used to disturb their general health and well-being. You're crossing the line into black magick if you're casting spells on people to cause them harm, or trying to bring misfortune on someone simply because you don't like them. These kinds of workings can be dangerous for all parties, and are the magickal equivalent of shooting oneself in the foot. Should the spell work, the victim will have to deal with obvious negative effects. The practitioner, however, could end up taking the brunt of the negativity as the energies they sent out — driven by the resentment and anger that fueled the spell — snap back to their source. The spell caster becomes the ultimate victim as they fall prey to their own hatred and bitterness. In the end, the minor inconvenience the spell causes the target is hardly worth the repercussions that the practitioner suffers as the spell backfires.

On the other hand, everyone has the right to defend themselves using whatever tools they have available. Magickal self-defense uses spells — sometimes of a darker nature — to counteract or eliminate harmful energies that are being directed at the practitioner. Many times, these spells concentrate on returning negativity to its sender, banishing, warding, and protection. While these workings can sometimes harm the target, the extent of damage done is a direct result of their own actions, and has nothing to do with the emotions or intent of the practitioner. The spell caster, in this case, is merely the catalyst for giving back what the target was dishing out in the first place. When done correctly, they never add their own negativity to the working, or ask for a specific misfortune to befall the aggressor. The target, however, will still be put in check, and the destructive activity will stop. Meanwhile, the practitioner can find peace without suffering the magickal side effects that might come with using blatant black magick.

The area between black magick and magickal self-defense is a touchy subject, because a witch must be able to use darker techniques in order to defend oneself. The simple truth is that not every situation can be dealt with using purely white magick. While it would be nice to live in a world where everyone plays nice, and no one ever lies or causes each other harm, we have to accept that not everyone follows the same moral code. Some people get a thrill from doing harm to others. Others are selfish, and only think about what they can get out of a world that they think owes them something. And others, still, are so lost and broken that the only way they know how to react to other people is with the same misery that they feel for themselves.

In such instances, these people don't understand that the harm they cause others creates a ripple effect that eventually leads back to them. They don't understand that their actions have consequences (or sometimes they do, and just don't care enough about others — or themselves — to change their behavior). In these situations, the practitioner must temporarily put aside their passiveness, and step into the mind of a magickal warrior. Just as a martial artist must know and use similar moves as his opponent to defeat him, sometimes an otherwise peaceful practitioner has to ward off harmful people or energies by using those same energies against them.

Even many shamans, who are considered great healers by their tribes and by anthropologists who study them, know the importance of learning both light and dark magick in order to be a fully functioning healer. In his article "Dark Side of the Shaman," ethnographer Michael Forbes Brown discusses how many shamans draw on the same power as so-called sorcerers in order to protect their tribes from sorcery, psychic attack, and illness. Many shamans believe that illnesses are caused by spirit darts that are sent out by sorcerers to cause harm to members of their tribe. Shamans, however, also possess these spirit darts, and can use them to counteract suspected attempts to curse a victim:

The sorcerer works in secret, using spirit darts to inflict suffering on his enemies. The shaman operates in the public eye and uses his own spirit darts to thwart the sorcerer's schemes of pain and untimely death. . . . Yet because shamans possess spirit darts, and with them the power to kill, the boundary between sorcerer and shaman is sometimes indistinct (169).

Like the shamans in the article, a modern witch should embrace both dark and light magick, and know when and how to use each one. The focus must be taken away from whether they're practicing "white" or "black" magick so that the witch can develop into a more balanced and well-rounded practitioner. Especially when it comes to using magick for self-defense, one must cast aside ideas that they will be magickally reprimanded for standing up for themselves in the face of an attack. Doing so will help any witch be ready for battle when they find themselves in tough situations.

In fact, many older generation shamans frown upon the one-sided practices of modern neo-shamans, and even those taught by Wicca and other New Age traditions. These traditions, sometimes for fear of being associated with Satan or other evil forces, shy away from the darker areas of their practice. For example, the modern day shaman trend — which is highly Americanized — tends to concentrate solely on healing, spiritual cleansing, and other purely positive workings. While these neo-shamans are definitely directing their energy into doing a great deal of good in peoples' lives, they're also watering down the true meaning of shamanism. As Brown explains:

New Age enthusiasts are right to admire the shamanistic tradition, but while advancing it as an alternative to our own healing practices, they brush aside its stark truths. For throughout the world shamans see themselves as warriors in a struggle against the shadows of the human heart. Shamanism affirms life but also spawns violence and death. The beauty of shamanism is matched by its power—

and like all forms of power found in society, it inspires its
share of discontent (171).*

The job of a shaman is to heal and protect his people. How can he
come to his tribe's defense if he's denying his darker powers? If he's
unable to connect with and utilize darker energies, he'll be useless against
threats such as spirit darts, illness, and counter sorcery from other tribes.
Elder shamans know that these powers are necessary for self-defense and
protection. In the same sense, learning to deal with bad people by turning
their own intentions against them is a fundamental part of successfully
practicing magick. Moreover, it's the essence of the darker magick
associated with the inverted mirror box. Once mastered, it's a potent, yet
passive, way of dealing with harmful people without getting your own
hands dirty.

The Dos and Don'ts of the Mirror Box

Like any other system of magick, the mirror box has certain rules
and warnings that need to be considered before trying the spells. Most
magickal rules are passed down from other experienced witches who have
learned from trial and error what causes different types of spells to yield
certain results. Other rules are based on common sense, or simple moral
responsibility for yourself and others.   Then there are rules that are
specific to the mirror box. Since the box works in a distinct way from
some other types of magick, it tends to carry its own set of dos and don'ts.
These are mostly things that I learned on my own — sometimes the hard
way — through my experiences with the spells in this book. I've included
them to give you an idea of how specific spells worked for me in hopes
that you'll know what to expect when using the spells I've provided, or
even when writing your own.

The most important magickal rule to remember is that no magickal
rule should be taken lightly. The rules are in place for a reason. They come
from the successes and failures of other witches throughout the ages, and

---

*From *Natural History*, November 1989. Copyright © Natural History Magazine,
Inc., 1989.

therefore represent invaluable wisdom to other followers of magickal paths. Practicing magick can bring amazing changes into the life of the practitioner on many levels. But it can also be used as a weapon, just like a gun. Spells can backfire just as easily as a gun in the wrong hands, too.

This is especially true with mirror magick, which tends to be stronger and more sensitive than some other kinds. A smart gun owner takes classes to learn gun laws, and how to responsibly load, handle, and shoot their weapon. Similarly, a smart practitioner always knows the rules of magick, as well as how to properly handle the magickal tool they're working with, and the energies needed to make it function. When taking on the responsibility of any working, it's important to follow the guidelines to avoid having your spell fail, or even worse, come back on you instead of your target.

That being said, these next few pages are not meant to scare you. The following list is a guide of rules that I feel are essential to know before attempting the spells in this book. This is by no means a complete list, but it does cover a great deal of what I've learned through experience. Each spell works in a different way, and will have different results. The outcome will depend greatly on the situation, the people involved, and the way in which the spell is executed. Also, you'll inevitably need to tailor a spell to a specific need that's not covered in this book, which will of course have a different outcome. Keep good notes of your work — and the results — so that you can add to this list as you gain more experience.

Aside from the two major magickal laws of Similarity and Contagion, there are some rules that could almost be considered laws themselves. Much like a law, there are rules that describe the way magick inherently is. No matter how it's used, or by whom, in certain situations the magick itself will always behave in the same way. However, these rules also instill wisdom in the practitioner as to how to behave *because* of the way magick works. Some magickal guidelines can therefore teeter on the edge of being a rule and a magickal law. I've come across many of these in the craft, but no matter what kind of working I'm doing, two of these rules always stand out:

Magick always follows the path of least resistance. Don't put anything in its way. When you cast a spell, the energies that you send out are on a mission. The intent you've put into the spell has charged those energies with a specific task. They already know where they're going, and what they're supposed to accomplish. As a natural course of action, these energies will follow the most open course of travel to achieve their goal. Your actions after you cast the spell can interfere with, or even ruin, the results. Therefore, it's important to take certain steps after a spell has been cast — both mundanely and magickally —to allow it to manifest with the best results, and in the best time.

For example, perhaps you've been arguing with a good friend for several weeks. You both usually get along great, and you just want things to get back to normal as quickly and smoothly as possible. You've tried to handle the situation mundanely by attempting to talk out your differences. But no matter what you say, your friend is holding on tight to their grudge. Since you've been getting a less than welcoming response, you cast a spell to bring peace between the two of you. Your friend, finally ready to talk, calls you the next day. The conversation starts out smooth, but quickly gets heated (after all, no one said the road to peace was free of pot holes). You both end up getting frustrated, and decide to end the call before things get out of hand. Instead of waiting until you've both cooled off to bring things up again, you immediately send a slew of off-color text messages. Just when your spell had started working to help you and your friend sort through your differences, your negative actions and impatience in the mundane world have put you right back where you started.

Another common mistake witches make is to cast several different spells to achieve the same goal. This usually happens when things aren't moving as fast as expected, or when the practitioner feels that their spell has failed. While it can definitely be hard to wait, it's vital to practice patience while waiting for your spells to manifest. If you start casting other spells on top of the original working, there is a good chance that signals will get crossed. This can cause the spells to give mixed — or even bizarre — results. Those involved might become confused or start acting out, which could end up causing more harm than good. It can also result in all of the spells breaking down completely, thereby yielding no results at all.

Think of it as continuing to click on an internet link that's taking too long to load. You click the link, and nothing happens. So you click it again ... and again. Then you hit the escape key a few times, trying to undo the last few clicks. Then you hit enter, thinking that might make it load faster. Had you been patient, the link might have already opened in its own good time. But, since you kept trying different tricks to get it to open, signals got crossed. The computer became confused. The website finally crashed under the jumble of mixed signals. You have no choice but to restart the machine altogether, leaving you frustrated, defeated, and farther behind than you were in the first place.

Throwing more magick at slower-working spells is no different. Even if you think you're helping matters along, it will only result in putting unnecessary blocks in your own path. If a spell seems to be taking a long time, there might be things going on in the background that are setting back the energies. While these blocks are probably unknown to you, the energies that you cast out are trying to work around those obstacles to get their job done. The last thing you want to do is set more roadblocks in the spell's path.

Always plan your workings carefully, even if it means analyzing every word and correspondence that you use. This is particularly true for spells and types of magick with which you're unfamiliar. If you've never made a mojo bag before, do some research so you understand how they work. If you've never used a Voodoo doll, make sure you know what you're getting into before you start stabbing needles into it. If you've never done a mirror box spell, read the book from cover to cover before you seal the lid over someone's hair. Even witches are only human, after all. Mistakes are easy to make. Be sure you've thought of everything before you cast. It may seem tedious at the time, but it will ensure that you're keeping the path clear for the magick to do its thing.

It happens in its own place, in its own time, and in its own way. Another funny thing about spells is that they almost never turn out the way you imagine. Despite your amazing visualization skills during the working, and no matter how hard you concentrate on a specific outcome, you can never guess exactly how or when a spell will manifest. If you do a spell for extra money, for example, it might come in the form of a raise at your job rather than that winning lottery ticket that you gamble for every

Wednesday. A spell to bring more love into your life could result in meeting a new best friend instead of the tall, dark lover you had in mind.

Similarly, a banishing or protection spell might take a problem person out of your life in an unexpected way. People who have caused me problems in the past have gotten expelled from school, fired from their jobs, and even put in jail shortly after I cast spells to get them off my back. However, my workings never specifically asked for these things to happen. I simply concentrated on taking their negativity off of myself, and sending it back toward them. My spells then took the natural course of action, based on the behavior of those people, to resolve the issues I was having with them.

Spells work this way because they're typically generalized to allow the energies to manifest in the best way possible. Spells for love or money usually involve bringing more of those energies into your life *in general* rather than causing someone to fall in love with you, or trying to win at gambling. Banishing spells often involve getting a person away from you *in general* instead of willing them to die, or asking that they befall some other kind of misfortune. Spells constructed in a more general way can work well, because they allow the energies to manifest in the quickest and most appropriate way that the situation warrants. While you can definitely be more specific in your workings, you have to take care not to cross other magickal lines that could impose on someone else's free will, or cause harm to another person either intentionally or accidentally. How specific you need to be will depend on the working, and, of course, on other people that it might effect.

Furthermore, the results of the same spell are almost never the same twice. Every person and situation is different, and any given spell will work in a unique way under different circumstances. I realized this when a good friend and I were both using the same mirror box spell on two different people that were giving us problems. At first, it seemed like his spell was working faster and more dramatically than mine. Within days of casting the spell, his target got fired for stealing from his job, broke the cell phone that he'd been using to harass my friend, and got shaken down for some money that he owed to the wrong people. All of the lying and backstabbing he'd been doing for the past few months was catching up to him fast.

Meanwhile, my spell seemed to be lagging behind. It also lacked the action that I was used to seeing with mirror box spells. This really irritated me at first — especially since I wrote the spell my friend was using, and his seemed to be working better than mine! Later, however, I learned that my target was indeed getting what they had coming to them. My target's results weren't as harsh, however, because that person wasn't involved in the same crooked lifestyle as my friend's target. I had to remind myself that my friend's situation was significantly more serious than mine, and would therefore see stronger results based on what his target had coming back to him.

In the end, the people in both of our boxes each learned their lesson in their own way. My friend's target ended up having to move to a different city, thereby banishing him permanently from his life. My target was driven to an almost tearful apology, which actually led to a reconciliation that we still honor today. All in all, my friend and I were both more than happy with the results of the same spell. We had to realize that because it was done on two different people — in two very different situations — it manifested in two completely different ways.

One thing I've learned is that you'll know it when you see it. While the results won't always yield a big show, you'll know by the events that *are* taking place that your spell has started to work. Keep your mind at ease, and let the spell work its magick in its own good time. Patience and persistence will allow the energies that you've sent out to bring about your desires. Cast your spell, then go about your life knowing that it's working the way it's supposed to according to the circumstances it has to work with.

Along with these two rules, there are other guidelines and bits of advice that apply more to mirror magick, which you'll want to keep in mind when performing the spells in this book. Study these carefully, and be sure to follow them vigilantly. If you find yourself questioning your motives before you cast a spell, refer to these rules to make sure you're on the right track. Avoid casting if you have even the slightest feeling that you might be stepping out of bounds. You might need to handle the situation in a different way (either with a different kind of spell, or by more mundane means).

Let your dreams guide you. Many witches have extremely vivid dreams that help guide them in their daily lives. For me, some dreams come across as actual events that happen later, while others come through as symbols that I recognize once I see them in real life. Most of these symbols repeat themselves in similar situations, so that I've come to learn their meanings over the years. For example, whenever I dream that someone I know has a demon face, I almost always find out that they are or were angry with me. Right before getting the news that two of my friends passed away, I had dreams that they went missing. I've even successfully predicted coworkers getting fired after dreaming about them getting in trouble right before it happened.

These dreams usually have a distinct feel that differentiates them from the normal stress dreams that we all have after a long day. Some people might even call them astral projections due to their realistic qualities. The air will feel thick and hazy. I can see, feel, smell, and hear almost better than I can in real life. In fact, everything will be so extremely vivid that when I wake up, I'm surprised to find myself in bed. Many times I can hear low, ambient music that sounds as if I've stepped between worlds, and the walls between the two dimensions are vibrating in my ears. I usually wake up thinking, *I hope you were paying attention, because you'll need that information later.*

The same dreams can sometimes give you clues as to the progress of spells that you've performed, and as to what might be going on behind the scenes. One of my most recent mirror box spells involved a supposed friend who I suspected of being two-faced after dreaming that he was showing everyone at a party the contents of my flash drive. Everyone in the dream was laughing at what they were reading on the screen as he pointed and led them on. Shortly after putting him in the box to find out what his true motives were, I started hearing that he wasn't who he pretended to be. Over the next couple of weeks it surfaced that he'd been showing my Facebook page to our mutual friends while making fun of a blog I was working on at the time, and also sharing our text messages and personal conversations with people I didn't even know.

The dream was letting me know in a symbolic way that he was sharing information that I had confided in him (the flash drive) with anyone and everyone who would listen (the other people at the party). Just as the dream portrayed, he was also using that information to make fun of me behind my back. All while sucking up to my face, and pretending to be a friend so he could gather more information to use against me. My truth spell was definitely working, and all while my dreams were revealing the true story behind my former friend's fake smile.

Your dreams might be substantially different, but they will still fit the situation that you're dealing with. For example, if you dream that your target is stuck inside the box, your spell has probably started to work. Dreams like the one I had about my two-faced "friend" will tell you how people are acting behind your back. If you've had someone in a box for quite some time, and you dream that they're weak or sick, it might be time to give them a break. Similarly, if you should have any kind of dream or vision about taking the box apart, it's time to let things rest. Following your dreams will help you figure out how the spell is manifesting, and also determine the next steps you should take to solve the problem.

Don't fret if you're not a big dreamer, or don't seem to remember your dreams easily. Everyone's brain works differently. You still have plenty of other instincts and senses that your spells will tap into to let you know how things are coming along. If you want to improve your dream-interpreting skills, keeping a dream journal is the best way to get started. Try to write your dreams down as soon as you wake up, and don't get discouraged if you can't remember many details right away. Many of the less vivid details can disappear from your memory in the time it takes to get ready for work in the morning. Being woken up suddenly by alarm clocks, loud noises, or the dreams themselves can also erase your memory of what happened.

Keeping a solid dream journal takes a good deal of discipline. Furthermore, learning to interpret your own dreams accurately comes with learning how your brain communicates certain symbols and events to your subconscious. Therefore, take special note of anything that comes true, and anything that repeats itself. Try to make connections between symbols that appeared in your dreams compared to what actually happened. You might find that similar symbols show up right before similar events take place, which will help you make more accurate predictions in the future.

Keep your intentions pure. If you cast a spell with bad intentions, the power will come back on you. Simple as that. This can be said for any spell, but is especially true with the mirror box, which is specifically designed to reflect those energies back on their sender. This can get particularly sticky when doing spells on difficult people. Spells of this nature deal with highly negative — sometimes even erratic — energies that can easily turn on the practitioner if done with the wrong objective. Most people can think of at least one person who really has it coming. Sometimes it's tempting to cast a spell that will cause them all the pain and heartache that you think they rightfully deserve. However, this crosses the line of sending out your own energies for the specific purpose of doing someone else harm.

As I've already mentioned, mirror box spells are meant to get harmful people off your back, and make them answer for what they did by making them face their own behavior. Only use these spells to stop and send back the same negative energy that the target is directing at you or others. To help you determine whether or not your intentions are pure, reexamine why you want to cast the spell in the first place. Then think about how the outcome will affect others, and how it might come back on you or them. If you're feeling any unwarranted anger or jealousy, or if you think the spell might do more harm than good, then don't do it. Try to solve the problem a different way, or do the spell at a later time when you can honestly say it's for the right reasons.

If you put someone in the mirror box for doing wrong, and it doesn't seem to be working, take a harder look at the situation. Does your target actually deserve to be in the box? Are they posing a real threat to you or someone else? Do you maybe have a grudge against them that's projecting your own thoughts or opinions unfairly onto that person? You must always be honest with yourself about your motives, and whether the target is actually doing something wrong. If they're innocent, the mirror box will only reflect back their actual qualities. They may even start having a long streak of good luck at the expense of the time and energy that you've put into the spell.

Don't add any extra negative energy to the spell. Along with keeping your intentions pure, you want to avoid adding unwanted energies to any spell. Casting a spell during an emotional storm is usually where witches get into trouble with this particular rule. Let's say you just got home from having lunch with your best friend, where a tearful confession was made that said friend has been sleeping with your partner behind your back. You're so livid that you almost didn't make it home without veering into a bus full of sweet little old ladies from the nursing home around the corner. As you slam your front door open, the only thing you can see is the white tunnel of pure rage that's taking over your line of sight. You can feel the anger coursing through your veins; heating your blood to the boiling point. Your teeth are clenched tight. Every muscle in your body is tensed up to the extreme. All you want to do is throw open your spell book, light a candle, and start stabbing away at that voodoo doll that you already have handy for situations just like this one. It only makes sense that the intense flood of rage you're feeling will add that much extra power to the spell, right?

Not necessarily. Although the energy coursing through you while you're angry is powerful, it's also highly destructive. The same is true when you're extremely depressed, crying, or otherwise highly emotional. Casting spells during an emotional storm can hinder the energy from flowing freely, and is another way that amplified negative energies can get sent back to you. Your emotions at the time will definitely get fed into the spell, but the results could be less than desirable. Even if you're extremely angry or hurt due to the actions of your target, always make sure you're calm and collected before you cast.

When working with mirror boxes, also make sure you're in a good emotional state when you touch the box or recite the verses. I can't stress enough that the point is to send back your target's own negativity, and not to attack them with your own. If you're unsure of your emotional state, try taking a few deep breaths, or doing a meditation to open your chakra centers. See how you feel after grounding the extra energy. You could also smudge your body with sage, or hold a quartz crystal while visualizing the stone taking the negative energy out of your body. If you still feel edgy, get the energy out with exercise such as jumping jacks, lifting weights, or boxing with a punching bag. Do whatever it takes to balance yourself out before beginning a spell.

One thing every magickal practitioner should know is that their thoughts are things. Witches must be careful what we think and say, because we know how to send our energies out to become real things and events in the physical world. Just like casting spells on top of spells, worrying that the spell isn't working (or that it might work in the wrong way) can actually cast that energy out against the original working. Your negative thoughts can break the spell down, which will lead to it manifesting in the wrong way (if it does at all). The best thing to do after you cast a spell is to go about your life, and let it work its magick. Most importantly, always remain positive about the outcome. Know that your energies are out there working as hard and as fast as they can to manifest your desires.

Never gloat. This is the surest way for your working to fall flat on its face. This rule applies to any situation, magickal or mundane, but is particularly true with magick. Gloating involves an array of negative emotions such as selfishness, pleasure at someone else's misfortune, and taking pride in having power over them. When brought into magick, these thoughts will be quick to come back on you (especially while others are watching).

Bragging about your spells brings unwanted attention from both believers and nonbelievers. Those who don't believe might pray for you and the person you did the spell on, which can break the spell you worked so hard to cast. Even if you don't believe in their religion — or in God at all — prayer of any kind is still a concentrated raising of power that gets directed through words and thoughts. Just like a spell, the person's will and desire set the energies in motion to manifest in the physical world. The result can break down the energies associated with your working, leaving you right back at the beginning.

Even if you only brag to other witches — people you think will be sympathetic to your cause — you never know which witch will know the person who's at the receiving end of your working. A friend of your target might find out, and then perform counter-magick to break your spell, or cast spells to protect your target from your influences. Even worse, your target might very well find out that you've been working magick against them, and by the time they do find out, the story will probably be so scrambled that not an inkling of truth will be left in the version that gets back to them.

I learned very early how quickly gloating can bring you down. When I was in middle school, I bragged to my friends about casting a spell on a teacher who I felt was singling me out in class. The spell was meant to take her attention off of me, and keep her mouth shut about me in front of my classmates. I had sealed the spell in an envelope, which I was carrying around in my backpack so that I would have it on me during class. I made the mistake of showing it to several people during lunch hour, and giving details about what it was supposed to do. Word quickly got around that I had "cursed" my teacher, and a rumor started that I was carrying a voodoo doll in my backpack that represented her. I was called into the administrator's office several days later. My backpack was searched, and the envelope containing the spell was confiscated. My teacher was informed of the "threatening" spell, and my mom was called away from work to come pick me up for the day.

The next few weeks were even more fun. Several of my teachers could barely look me in the eye. One moved me to the front of the class so she could keep a better eye on me. Another one invited me to his church. Rumors were going around that I worshiped Satan, and that I was responsible for the death of a student who had passed away earlier that year. Other students were asking me if I could fly. They wanted to know if I would curse people that they didn't like. The principal was keeping a solid eye on me, too. She wouldn't let me wear certain colors or necklaces, and even pulled me aside during lunch to turn a t-shirt inside out, because it had a logo with flames printed on it. I became the cause of total witch hysteria at my middle school for the remaining two months of the school year.

I did get what I wanted in the end (after finding out about the spell in my backpack, that particular teacher definitely left me alone), but not in the way that I wanted. Rather than my teacher backing off because the spell peacefully compelled her to do so, she was leaving me alone because she was afraid of me. I also had to deal with the other rumors that were being spread by ignorant people who didn't understand witchcraft, and who were letting their imaginations and religious beliefs get the best of them. While my spell ultimately did work, my bragging ended up causing me a great deal of trouble. Had I kept quiet about the working, I feel that it would have worked just fine on its own, and without all the commotion that my mouth had started. Things were pretty much forgotten by the time I got back to school the following year (although, years later, I did run into one of my teachers at a restaurant. She pulled me aside, and whispered in my ear, "so, are you still a *witch*?"), but I definitely learned my lesson about bragging to other people about my spells.

Another way witches get in trouble with gloating is by carrying a smug attitude about their practice. I've met my fair share of people who claim to be more powerful than others, or claim to be the supreme authority on witchcraft. I've also heard witches brag about doing spells to harm other people, and have seen some use their knowledge of witchcraft to manipulate and abuse others. One thing I've yet to see is any of these people keep friends (or power) for very long. While they may be able to pull one over on newer witches for a while, most people wizen up, realize their own power, and either move on to a more supportive group, or end up practicing as solitaries. Those who are pretentious about their practice, or use it as a tool for manipulation, usually end up isolated from other witches who have a desire to learn and grow from other practitioners.

On the other side of the coin, discussing workings that you've done with like-minded individuals (after those spells are done and over with) is perfectly acceptable. Most witches share spells and ideas in order to grow spiritually, and to expand the scope of magickal abilities at their disposal. This book is a good example. In this work, I'm sharing my spells, and the results that I perceived after casting them, in order to educate other practitioners on how the mirror box works, and to help them learn how to use this powerful magickal tool. My stories are testimonials that I feel back up the spells and theories that I've shared. What I haven't done is call anyone out by name in order to slander or embarrass them, nor have I taken pride in causing harm to another person by means of witchcraft, or claimed to be more powerful than anyone else (witch or not). It's crucial to remain respectful and humble with everyone you meet. Every practitioner must be careful not to fall into trash-talking, belittling or abusing others, or putting themselves on a pedestal that they will inevitably crash down from.

Be prepared for some backlash when you first cast a spell. In my experience (and the experience of other friends who have tried the mirror box) the person in the box can feel on a psychic level that something is working against them. Sometimes they can even sense the source of the energy. They may find themselves angry with you for no reason, and might get confrontational with you or others. A certain degree of hostility is a normal reaction on the part of the target, and is something I've seen happen more than once. I've had to learn to let them suffer through it until they come to terms with the fact that whatever misery they're experiencing is what they're putting themselves through based on how they treat others.

If you're dealing with someone who's dangerous, or who has a great deal of bad energy heading back their way, it never hurts to cast a protection spell over yourself and your property. Whenever possible, you should also take steps in the mundane world to distance yourself from that person until the spell has run its course. Sometimes they end up being banished from your life anyway, but this won't always be the case. There are times when it won't be as simple as banishing someone (if, for instance, you have a close personal or professional relationship with them). If necessary, block that person in your phone, on social media, and on any other platforms that they could use to contact you. Steer clear of them as much as possible until the spell has done its job.

Should things start getting too exciting for your comfort, take the box apart and give the spell a rest for a few days, a week, or even a moon cycle. A good look in the mirror might be just what they needed to straighten up, and their behavior may stop once the spell is closed. If the person does continue to act horribly afterward, feel free to place them back in the box for another week to moon cycle.

For added protection, you can reword your spells to keep the person on their own side of the fence while they're in the box. Don't be afraid to cast the spell just because the target might not be able to handle what gets thrown back at them. As they say: if you can't take it, then don't dish it out. Just be sure to protect yourself while the spell is running its course.

Try not to leave anyone in the box for too long. The mirror box is similar to mojo bags, witch jars, and voodoo dolls in that it's a physical representation of the working. The energies associated with the spell are attached to and driven by these objects, and can continue to act on the target long after the point has been made. Even if the working doesn't cross your mind for some time, spells of this nature don't typically end once they've completed their task. As long as the tool used as the vehicle of the spell still exists, the target can continue to be bombarded by the energies of the working. Those energies could then start coming back on the practitioner in strange ways if they're causing your target unnecessary distress or hardship.

Another side effect is that the energies will stagnate, thereby making the spell go stale. If you set the mirror box aside for six months without paying attention to it, the spell can get stuck in a kind of limbo (the energies find themselves somewhere between working toward a goal that has already been accomplished, and waiting for the spell to end). For this reason, it's necessary to tie up your magickal loose ends by ritually dismantling the box, and destroying its contents. Doing so signals the definitive end to the spell. Furthermore, it allows the energies to be neutralized so that they can dissipate, and return to the universe to serve other purposes. Most importantly, you and your target will be taken out from under the influence of the spell, allowing both of you to return to your normal lives. Pay close attention to how your mirror box spells are coming along — and how long they've been active — so that you know when it's time to bring them to a close.

Determining how long is too long will depend greatly on both the situation and the nature of the spell. In my experience, mirror spells tend to work rather quickly. If you see the results you were after in one or two weeks, then you should end the spell at that time. More stubborn circumstances might require more time and energy. A good way to handle these situations is in moon cycles. For example, if you started the spell on the new moon, but you still haven't gotten the results you wanted by the next new moon, take the box apart and let things rest for a week or few. If things haven't worked themselves out by that time, give the spell another shot. Casting spells in cycles not only gives things time to rest between workings, but it continually refreshes the energies so they don't go stagnant.

If you feel that your spell didn't work, or it didn't work out the way you wanted it to, look at the situation from a different perspective. Also look at how you worded and performed the spell. It might be necessary to rethink your strategy. You might have cast a perfectly good spell, but maybe it didn't quite fit the situation. There will also be cases where someone straightens up while they're in the box, but then goes right back to their typical behavior after the spell has been lifted. Don't hesitate to give them another round in the box if they start causing you more problems.

Always end one spell before starting another of a similar nature. This goes back to the idea of casting multiple spells on top of each other. It's perfectly normal for a witch to have more than one working going on at the same time. They might have one kind of protection spell over their house, another on their car, and might be wearing a mojo bag to attract prosperity while carrying a stone in their pocket to keep their lover faithful. Doing so is perfectly acceptable, because all of these spells are meant to remedy a variety of situations. It's unlikely that the signals will get crossed, because the energies are all performing specialized tasks on several different frequencies.

The problem lies in casting multiple spells to the same end. One spell per situation at a time is sufficient. Give your spell time to work before you start another toward the same goal. If you feel that a spell has failed, or you didn't get the results you wanted, always ritually end the first spell before starting another one. As always, keep good notes so you can see where things might have gone wrong, or where you could improve the spell to make the results more precise next time you use it.

Furthermore, it's always a good idea to let things rest a bit between spells. The power behind a working can have a huge effect on those involved. Giving your target — or the situation in general — a break gives everyone a chance to breathe, and gives the situation itself a chance to finish working itself out. You might even notice that bringing the spell to an end is just what the working needed to finish up the job. Depending on how much of a hurry you're in, this break can be a few days to an entire moon cycle. If you're still experiencing problems after a moon cycle, then you can consider recasting the spell, or even doing a different one that will have more precise results.

Start over if the box gets cracked or broken in any way. I've only had one mirror box break since I've been doing these spells. I was in the midst of shaking the box to refresh the original spell when it slipped out of my hand, and hit the wall on the other side of the altar. The tape around the edges held the broken pieces in place, but the box was cracked on three sides. I took that as a sign that either the spell had done its thing, or that my target needed a break. I made the decision to ritually destroy the box so that any residual energies attached to the spell would be stopped from taking further action. I then waited to see how things played out with my target.

I soon learned that my target had been going through an extremely difficult time dealing with some issues in their personal life. These issues were completely unrelated to my spell, and were actually already going on before I cast it. Nevertheless, what my target was going through was hard to deal with, and the events taking place were actually causing a shift in their conscience as far as how they had been treating people. I still believe to this day that my spell ended itself for two reasons. First of all, I feel that it ended because the energies that were being sent back (even though they were that person's own doing) were too much for them to deal with at that time. I also feel that my target was already honestly working to make positive changes, and therefore the spell was both unnecessary and excessive.

What happened in this case is a good example of why some spells just don't work. We never know every detail about what's going on in the background, and there will be times when a spell fails because it's not in the best interest of everyone involved. You might believe that this is the universe stepping in to end it, or some other outside force reminding you that you've overstepped your bounds. I believe that the energies simply don't work well with the situation, and are unable to get around the blocks being put in their path. Whatever the case, when a mirror box breaks, try to take that as a sign that you might not have had all the information you need, and that there might be things going on at that particular moment that are more important than your spell. Keep your heart and mind open so that your spells can communicate back to you how things are working. They might even tell you in a big way that it's time to back off for a while.

Know the entire situation before taking action. We've all been in situations where someone caused trouble for us by spreading rumors, or by blaming us for something we didn't do. Just as you would want the benefit of the doubt if someone were putting you in that position, you should always do others the same favor. Try not to get worked up over things you've heard from others, but focus instead on things you've actually seen with your own eyes, and heard with your own ears. Investigate rumors and gossip before immediately throwing the suspected troublemaker into a mirror box. It could be that people are spreading rumors about them, too, and they're just as frustrated as you are. If someone seems like they're doing something behind your back, but you can't quite prove it, try having a respectful conversation with them about the situation. If a good heart to heart is out of the question, try a truth spell to see what's going on out of earshot. You'll be amazed at how much information falls into your lap with a little magickal help.

Sometimes friends — and even family members — will try to stir up trouble and turn you and other friends or relatives against each other. Jealousy is usually the motivation here. Maybe a new person has come into your life, and a friend or relative feels that you're being taken away from them. They could be trying to drive the new person out of your life in order to "protect what's theirs" so that they don't lose you. Anger is another common reason that people spread rumors or start trying to pit people against each other. Even sheer boredom will lead people to start gossip or arguments for their own entertainment. Whatever the reason, actions like these can cause serious problems that break up friendships and relationships, when in reality nothing major was happening. If you've found yourself in this situation, try to get to the bottom of things before taking action. Be sure you're putting the blame where it actually belongs so that innocent people don't continue to get hurt in the crossfire.

Putting someone in the mirror box for something they didn't do will result in the spell not working at all, which is a huge waste of your valuable time and energy. It could also lead to unnecessary negative energy being directed at that person, and in turn back at you. Always know the entire situation before casting any spells, especially ones of this caliber. Casting spells haphazardly attracts bad energy, wastes your own energies, and results in bad practice that will ultimately set you back in your development as a practitioner.

Leave your target alone after the spell has worked. As I stated before, it's important to take the box apart after the spell has done its job. Keeping someone in the box after you've seen the results you wanted can cause magickal overkill by keeping the spell working against them after it runs its course. This, in turn, can cause excess stress in that person's life that can begin to come back on you in various ways.

Once the spell has worked, it's time to leave your target alone. That could mean getting an apology, seeing them back off from harassing you, or that particular person being banished from your life completely. No matter what, you must both go on about your lives in order to keep that separation between you, and to maintain the peace that the spell created. This counts even more for the practitioner, since the spell that you performed created a link between the two of you at the time it was cast. Keeping the energy flowing via the mirror box keeps them tied to you on a spiritual level. It wouldn't make sense to go out of your way to cross paths with someone after you've put a restraining order on them. For the same reason, it doesn't make sense to perform a spell to banish someone, then fail to sever the magickal bond between you once the spell has manifested successfully.

Take the box apart once you've seen the results you wanted. Then forget about it. Try to put that person out of your mind completely. If the activity ceases, you can be happy knowing that you did good work. Should their negative behavior start back up again, it might be necessary to repeat the spell. No matter what, once they stop harassing you, the spell should be ended so that everyone involved can go back to living their own lives.

Know when to accept an apology (if you get one). Every now and then the best course of action of a mirror box spell is that the target actually feels remorse for what they did wrong. Rather than banishing them from your life, the spell might result in that person wanting to apologize to you. You must remember that, although this might not be the result you were after, it was the best way for the spell to manifest considering the situation and the people involved.

As I've already mentioned, I had to learn this for myself when one of my own mirror box spells ended in an almost tearful apology from my target. I was still angry at the time, and was having a great deal of trouble taking it seriously. I was also frustrated because I wasn't getting the usual action-packed results that I was used to seeing at other times I'd done the spell. I remember thinking to myself as I was taking the box apart, *well, that was nice. But what about everything I went through? Is that really it?*

While I didn't feel like the spell was a complete failure, I did think at first that the results were mediocre. I was concerned that my target would go right back to their hateful ways after I accepted the apology, thinking that it would be that easy to win me over every time they did something to disrespect me. Later, however, I was surprised to see that my target was making an honest effort to stay on good terms with me. I could tell that there was actual remorse for the problems that had been caused. Although our friendship has never quite been the same, the spell did put things into perspective for both of us in a way that has allowed us to respect each other's boundaries. We were able to agree to disagree on many things, and we still get along just fine to this day.

Furthermore, this particular spell made me think back on times in which I myself had to apologize for doing someone wrong. I remembered how hard it was to acknowledge that you hurt someone, and to tell them that you were wrong. Even worse, I remembered how hard it is when someone denies your honest efforts to reconcile. I eventually came to appreciate the apology as the best way that the spell could have turned out. After all, it's always better to come out of these situations as friends rather than enemies.

Of course, not all of your workings are going to have such a happy ending. Many people are too stubborn to apologize, or are too submersed in their own anger and resentment to even consider trying to get along with you. It might even be that you're the one holding on to extra emotional baggage, and don't think that the target is worth the trouble of a reconciliation (and there will definitely be times when they indeed are not). Let your spell work in its own way, and it will handle these people and situations in the most appropriate manner.

Should you receive an apology, accept it with an open heart and mind. However, keep in mind what that person did to you. Forgiving and forgetting are definitely two different things. Make sure the other person understands your personal boundaries, and exactly what it means to cross those lines. The hardest part — particularly when dealing with relatives, or someone you would still like to consider a friend — is learning to forgive without leaving yourself open to further mistreatment or manipulation. Only time and loyalty will really prove a person's motives. Respect yourself first, then demand that same respect from others. No matter what.

Constructing the Mirror Box

Basic Supplies and Correspondences

The most important part of mirror box magick is, of course, the box itself. Which way the mirrors face, the size and shape of the mirrors used, and other things you add to the box all play a role in how the spell will work. Thankfully, many of the necessary supplies are readily available in craft stores and supermarkets. You might even already have a lot of the materials you need lying around the house. Even better, they're extremely cheap to make. Depending on how fancy you want to get, a basic mirror box can usually be put together for less than five dollars (cheaper than certain candles you might use for other types of spells).

From the mirrors themselves to the different correspondences that go into the box, the final cost of your working will depend entirely on the quality of the supplies that you use. Fresh herbs can always be replaced with dried. The same herbs mixed with a little olive or vegetable oil can be used in place of their essential oil counterparts. Twenty-five-cent candles will do the same job as seven-dollar candles. There are even substitutes for the mirrors when they (or funds to buy them) aren't readily available. As with any working, a little creativity and ingenuity will pave the way to the perfect spell every time, regardless of the price tag on the items used.

The primary components of the mirror box are the box itself, a personal effect that represents the target, and several correspondences that match the theme of the spell. Secondary components are what you use to seal the box, symbols that you draw on the inside or outside to add extra power, and where you store the box while the spell is running its course. There are many options for all the different parts. How they're combined and how they interplay is what makes the spell. This chapter will take you through every step of building the perfect mirror box. The finished product can be used for any spell in this book, as well as any spell that you write on your own in the future.

As you hunt for supplies, keep a running list of where you bought each item. Keep track of where you found the best deals so you can go back when it's time to make another box. As you gain more experience with mirror box spells, you'll likely come to prefer certain mirrors, herbs, or other items that you've used to make your spells your own. Always make note of where you found your favorite items so you can find them again later. Also keep good notes of different substitutes you use, and how the spells worked out in the end.

The Mirrors

The first step to building the ideal mirror box is finding the best mirrors to fit your needs. I usually buy mirrored tiles from the craft store. They come in several shapes and sizes, but, usually, the smaller you go, the more mirrors you get per package for the same price. Remember that the finished box needs to be big enough to hold a personal effect of the person (either something they once touched or owned, their photo, a body bit, or a slip of paper with their name written on it), a few herbs or charms that correspond to the spell, and any other items you come across that you want to use. It's a good idea to always plan out what you'll use, and gather those items before you buy the mirrors so that you pick the right size for your specific needs.

Also keep in mind that some of the mirrors might be chipped or cracked when you open the package. This is an unfortunate side effect of shipping and handling that's sometimes unavoidable. I stick with medium-sized mirrors so that I get a package that contains more than six. That way,

I'll have several to choose from in case one or two are too damaged to use. I'll even buy more than one package to cover all my bases, and to ensure that I have extra mirrors on hand for my next spell.

Another — although more expensive — option is to buy six square mirrors that are already framed. Locker, bathroom, or small deco mirrors all make good candidates. The existing frames on these mirrors make for stronger boxes that hold up better to being dropped or accidentally thrown while shaking. However, they also tend to be bigger and bulkier, which will make it more difficult to fit the finished box on your altar, or hide it in a safe place. The smaller mirrors at the hobby store are more inconspicuous, and much easier to keep out of the way.

Sometimes, for whatever reason, mirrors just won't be available. When money is tight, or the hobby store is closed on a Sunday, you'll have to find another way to construct the box — or at least simulate the action of the spell. The following substitutes will help you cast your spells with items you might have easier access to, or probably already have on hand. Have no fear if your search for mirrored tiles finds you at a dead end. Your spells can still be performed using the alternatives on the following list.

Tin foil: Tin foil is, in my opinion, the best substitute when mirrors are unavailable. It's cheap, easy to work with, and probably in your kitchen right now. I've seen this done several ways. What worked best for me was to find a small cardboard box, and line the side I wanted to use with the foil. Matchbooks work well if your other supplies will fit inside. A friend of mine repurposes the Birchboxes from her beauty subscription to use as mirror boxes.

If you can't find an existing box, you can cut six equal squares out of a piece of cardboard, then glue the tin foil to one side of each square. Construct the box with the cardboard tiles just as you would with the mirrors, then cast the spell as usual. Another option is to lay the foil out on your workspace, and place the contents that would usually go inside the box in the center of the foil. Where you would normally seal the box shut, you instead wrap or ball up the foil as a tight package that surrounds the contents on all sides. When it's time to end the spell, instead of taking it apart like you would the mirror box, you ritually dispose of the entire package by burying it.

Plastic rearview mirror: Sometimes you just won't be able to find the mirrors you need to make a box. The hobby store might be out, or the one in your town might not carry them. In this case, try the auto parts store, or the auto section at your local big box store. You should be able to find sheets of plastic mirror that are used to replace broken rearview mirrors. These can be cut into six equal-sized squares that will work perfectly to construct the box. Plastic mirrors will result in a flimsier finished product, so extra care needs to be taken when handling the box, or the plastic mirrors will need to be glued to cardboard to make it sturdier. The obvious upside to using plastic is that the box can't be smashed if it accidentally gets dropped.

Compact mirror: The compact works on the same principle as an inverted mirror box: you seal the person inside so that the energies they put out reflect back on them. A compact with a mirror on both sides works best, since it simulates the action of them being surrounded on all sides. If all you have is a compact with a mirror on the top and makeup on the bottom, be sure to put your personal effect (such as the person's photo) facing up toward the mirror.

Wrong sized mirrors: One problem I ran into the first time I tried to build a mirror box was that I was trying to use mirrors that were the wrong shape and size. I was using rectangular tiles, which made an awkward, oversized box with a lid that sank down in the center. The lid also hung over the edges a little so that it chipped easily, and was therefore dangerous to handle. To solve the problem, I turned to the idea of making my own box out of cardboard. I made six squares big enough that I could glue a mirror to the center of each one, then put them together to form the box. You could also repurpose an existing cardboard box if one is available. This will work with any small mirrors that are awkward sizes, or the wrong shape to make a square box.

An existing mirror box: When I performed my "Wake Up and Smell the Coffee" spell, I actually used a mirror box that a friend had given me as a gift. It was already lined with mirrors on the inside, was painted black on the outside, and had a pewter Celtic dragon embedded on the lid. Some music and jewelry boxes are made in much the same way. If you happen to have something like this around the house, and the mirrors face the way you need them to, feel free to use it instead of spending the time and cash to make one from scratch.

If you have an existing mirror box that you want to use, but the mirrors are facing the wrong way, you can sometimes rewrite the spell so that the working fits what you have on hand. For example, if you need to banish someone, but the mirrors only face outward, you could instead write the spell to protect yourself from that person's influences. Doing so will spiritually block that person from doing harm against you, which is the equivalent of banishing their influences from your life. Similarly, if you want to perform a working to deflect social anxiety, but the mirrors only face inward, perform the spell to reflect more self-confidence instead.

The Personal Effect

The second most important ingredient in a successful mirror box spell is the personal effect. As I discussed in chapter one, this is the link to the target that directs the energy of the spell directly to that person. The best personal effect is a body bit, which is something that was once part of the target. Hair, fingernail clippings, a q-tip covered in earwax, chewed up pen caps, old gum, or something else coated with their saliva are all good options. Other bodily fluids and waste have been used by witches in the past. By no means do I personally suggest this. Bodily fluids can be dangerous to handle. Not to mention that what you might have to do to get them can be both disturbing and illegal. Try to stick with cleaner and easier-to-obtain bits, and keep in mind that some of them are biohazardous waste. Always handle these personal effects with as much care as you would any other bodily refuse.

Even the safer body bits can be extremely hard to get your hands on (particularly if the target is someone you're not close to such as your manager at work or an enemy). When an actual part of the person's body is unavailable, try to at least get something that they've touched. Following the Law of Contagion, anything they've laid their hands on will have a permanent spiritual link to them. Stick to things that are small enough to fit inside the box. Coins, pen caps, a sample of their handwriting or signature, et cetera will all work fine. Avoid handling these items excessively, as you don't want too much of your own energy getting attached to them. Try to keep your findings in a small black pouch or bandana until the time comes to cast the spell.

A photograph of the target is another excellent "body bit" that can be placed inside the box. A photo is a representation of a person's unique image. It's the face that everyone they know recognizes when they see them. A person's picture tends to evoke their name when friends, family, and even enemies see it. It can also evoke the feelings that those people hold in their hearts for that person. Therefore, it represents a direct spiritual link to them that can be used to send out the energies cast in a spell.

A few decades ago, photos could be hard to find if you weren't connected to the person rather intimately. But in today's world of Facebook, Twitter, and other social media, you can usually get a photo of your target at the click of your mouse. When you can get one, always write the person's name on the back. Be sure to pick out or print a photo small enough that it will fit inside the box. If you end up having to fold it to make it fit, always do so at least three times.

Let's say you've tried getting a few stray hairs off the cushion of your manager's office chair, but with no luck. You tried snagging his favorite pen before the day was over, but he guards it with his life. You even hoped to sneak a photo off of his Facebook page, but he deleted his account a few weeks ago to avoid another coworker who keeps stalking his profile. It seems like the universe has left you empty-handed on your search for the tiny personal link needed to guide the spell in the right direction. You need to get your hands on something, so what do you do now?

Just use your target's name. A person's name *is* their identity. They answer to it when people call it out loud. They use it to buy everything from a tank of gas to the house in which they live. Everything they've ever done is attached to that name. Even after they die, their name will continue to identify them in the thick letters etched across their headstone. The memories they shared with their friends and relatives will run through people's minds as they stand before that gravestone and read the name out loud. So, when all else fails, just write their name on a slip of paper with a pen, fold it three times, and toss it in the box.

In fact, the target's name on a slip of paper is the default personal effect used for every spell in this book. It's the easiest to get your hands on. Not to mention the least invasive, and least likely to get you in trouble for stalking behind your enemy, waiting for little crumbs to fall so you can collect them. Even when I do luck out enough to get a lock of hair or something that they've touched, I still like to write their name on a slip of paper and call it out several times. Doing so puts that person's image in my mind during the spell, and helps me make a stronger connection with them. Then I can better focus my energy towards them as I carry out the working.

All the better if you can find several of these items. The more links you have to the target, the stronger the connection to them will be. Just remember to be careful when trying to obtain these personal effects. Never do anything illegal, or anything that will harm the person in the process. No going into their house uninvited. No cutting out chunks of their hair, and running away. No tackling them, and beating them in the back of the head until they spit out their gum. Be safe, be smart, and be slick. Otherwise, you might find yourself casting a whole new set of spells to convince a judge to let you go back outside without supervision.

Herbs, Candles, and Other Correspondences

After you have a good personal effect picked out, you can choose a few herbs, oils, or other correspondences that fit the type of working you're doing. One question that outsiders — and even many experienced witches — sometimes have is, "why does this herb or stone supposedly have this power?" There are many things that determine how correspondences come to be associated with certain powers or qualities. Almost all of them, however, point back to a concept known as the Doctrine of Signatures. Based heavily on the Law of Similarity, the Doctrine of Signatures is the ancient belief that certain herbs, stones, and other natural elements of our environment are marked with a signature (be it their shape, color, smell, or even the area in which they're found) that gives a clue as to the medicinal or magickal use of that plant or object.

This idea dominated early herbal medicine and lore, and is the source of many popular remedies that are still in use today.

Popular examples are that walnuts bear a close resemblance to the human brain. Therefore, they were thought to help with ailments of the brain and mind. Kidney beans look like kidneys, so they're used to help the kidneys function properly. Ginger root, which is shaped like the human stomach and intestines, is used to treat many gastrointestinal complaints. Similarly, spicy herbs like cayenne pepper have been used to treat fevers because of their heat.

While some may scoff at the Doctrine of Signatures as pure conjecture, they fail to realize that many of these herbal remedies have been scientifically proven. Some of them have even been turned into pharmaceutical drugs that treat everything from headaches to cancer. Willow bark, for example, is the source of salicylic acid — the main ingredient in Aspirin, many acne treatments, and other anti-inflammatory medicines. Turmeric, another herb known for its anti-inflammatory qualities, is currently being studied for its ability to shrink cancerous tumors. In fact, medical researchers have derived many of their treatments from traditional herbal remedies still used by traditional healers in tribes throughout the world.

The Doctrine of Signatures can be just as useful in magick as it is in medicine. The same principle helped link many herbs, stones, and other correspondences to their magickal uses. Some of the associations came from different properties of a certain herb or plant. Thorny plants such as burrs and roses are said to ward off evil influences. Many fragrant or colorful herbs and flowers, which stimulate feelings of pleasure, have come to be associated with love or passion. Chrysanthemum and other flowers that typically bloom in the fall — the time when many cultures hold their death festivals — have come to be associated with death and the afterlife. Similarly, mistletoe and poinsettia have connections to winter festivals in several traditions.

Other correspondences came about based on colors. Black is the color typically associated with darker workings such as protection and warding. Therefore, black items such as black pepper, snowflake obsidian, lampblack, and black candles have all come to be associated with these spells. The energy of love is typically associated with red and pink, which means that roses, red or pink candles, rose quartz, and rubies can all be used in love spells. To take it to the next level, since hearts are associated with love, anything that's shaped like a heart can also be associated with love. Even a simple heart cut out of a piece of paper can carry a strong symbolic association in a love spell.

Sometimes, however, the link between two things might not be as obvious. Many associations between objects and their purposes were made simply because they seem to vibrate at a similar frequency on a metaphysical level. A lot of witches do this, choosing what "just feels right" when they put a spell together, and letting intuition tell them what would be best for a certain spell or situation. This is a perfectly acceptable way to pick out correspondences that some witches actually rely on to guide them through the process of creating the perfect spell.

Some spells will have a theme, which will make it more obvious which correspondences can be used. I used coffee beans in my "Wake Up and Smell the Coffee" spell not only for their strong aroma and color, but also because of the association with the idiom that I used as the overall theme. The play on words made for a good correspondence pun that gave focus to the spell, and helped me visualize exactly what I wanted to happen while I was casting it.

Finally, there are those correspondences that are considered good, old-fashioned standbys. These are typically learned from herbal lore, word-of-mouth, and other witches throughout time. Some examples are basil for protection, roses for love, black pepper for banishing, and sage for spiritual cleansing. These correspondences continue to work well for other witches, and have therefore become ingrained in the craft as traditional options. Since they get passed from one witch to another without much contradiction, correspondences like these tend to be fairly static from one book of shadows to another.

You probably already have a list of favorite correspondences that have worked well for you over time. Depending on your level of experience, you've likely come to prefer certain herbs, stones, or candle colors in certain situations. Like magick itself, correspondence lists aren't meant to be black and white. No list of correspondences in any book is, by any means, the be-all and end-all of magickal knowledge. They're simply suggestions based on the experiences of witches of the past and present of things that tend to vibrate at similar frequencies. If you prefer to use blue for love instead of red, then go for it. If you find apples better than lemons for truth spells, then use those instead. Draw on your own instincts and experiences to make existing correspondence lists more complete, or more relevant to your personal practice. And, as always, be sure to keep good notes of what worked for you and what didn't so that you can refer back to those notes later.

An interesting fact about correspondences is that they can drastically change depending on the cultural background of the practitioner. The perception of a group of people can completely change their set of correspondences based on their experiences in daily life. Money correspondences are a perfect example. Paper money in the United States is typically green, so this color is usually associated with money spells on our side of the globe. However, other countries have silver, gold, blue, and even brown money. Witches in other countries might use these colors in their money spells instead of green, since this is their cultural perception of money. Similarly, where Americans typically wear white to weddings to symbolize the purity of the bride, in China a wedding dress is usually bright red to symbolize prosperity and love in the marriage. The most important thing is that the connection is made in the mind of the spell caster between the energies being invoked, and the desired outcome being petitioned. Whatever brings the idea of a certain energy to mind when you cast a spell is what you should use to bring the working to life.

All that being said, the following tables list possible herbs, stones, colors, and symbols to use in different workings. Although I'm not usually picky about moon phases and planetary influences, I understand that many witches religiously plan their workings by them. Therefore, I've also suggested the best moon phases and planetary energies to use when performing different types of spells. Since days are said to be ruled by planets, I've also included the best days to perform specific spells. Again, these are all options that you can use to add your own flair to the spells in this book, or to help write your own as the need arises. By no means do you have to use the information that I've included, nor do you have to include one thing from every category in your spell. But if you're the type of person who likes to cover all their bases, it definitely couldn't hurt.

One thing that's crucial, however, is to pay special attention to which way the mirrors face for each type of working. The mirrors are the catalyst for the action of the spell. If you cast a spell to send back negativity, but put your own name in an inverted mirror box, you might accidentally end up casting a return to sender spell on yourself. When deciding which way you want the mirrors to face, think about whether you're trying to reflect or deflect energies, and whether you want them to come back to, shine off of, or be sent away from the target. I give some suggestions in the correspondence tables, as well as at the beginning of each spell. Keep in mind that every situation will be different. The battle you're fighting might not fit what I've written, and will therefore require a little more creativity on your part. Follow your intuition, and let each situation tell you how the spell should be written to fit your needs.

BANISHING

Mirrors: Inward to make negative influences reflect back on the target, which usually drives them away from the practitioner. Outward to protect a target from negative influences or situations, and to keep them from affecting the target.

Colors: Black.

Herbs: Basil, black pepper, calamus, clove, dragon's blood, garlic, High John the Conqueror root, mugwort, myrrh, patchouli, rosemary, sage, thyme, valerian.

Day: Saturday.

Planet: Saturn.

Moon Phase: New to full for protection from a negative person or influence. Full to take the most power over the influence. Full to new to actively drive it away.

Elements: Air to carry away the evil influences (tornado charms work well with this element), to banish evil thoughts, and to create magickal force fields. Earth to stop evil in its tracks, and to provide safety for the victim. Fire to create magickal force fields, and to burn out evil energies. Water to wash away negative emotional influences, and purify the victim of any damage done.

Stones: Black onyx, clear quartz, hematite, obsidian, red jasper, smoky quartz, tiger's eye.

Symbols: Brooms, counterclockwise spirals, crosses, horns of Cernunnos (made with the hands), pentacles, snakes, Xs.

BREAKING SPIRITUAL BLOCKS AND ADDICTIONS

Mirrors: Inward to place appropriate restrictions on yourself concerning food, alcohol, drug use, and other addictions. Can also be used for inner reflection to force yourself to face problems you don't want to see. Outward to banish the desire to continue using an addictive substance or acting on an addictive habit. Helps break spiritual blocks, creative blocks, and ruts in general by deflecting and banishing thoughts and energies that can cause setbacks.

Colors: Black, dark blue, dark red.

Herbs: Almond, black pepper, calamus, citrus fruits, dandelion root, dragon's blood, High John the Conqueror root, licorice root, milk thistle, sage, sassafras, valerian.

Day: Saturday.

Planet: Saturn.

Moon Phase: New to full to find the strength to overcome addictions, move past obstacles, and be able to walk away from people or situations that stand in your way. Full to break ties with addictions for good, and to clear your path of negative spiritual roadblocks. Full to new to banish your desire to continue in negative addiction patterns, and to banish thoughts and energies that cause setbacks and ruts.

Elements: Air to release your mind of negative thought patterns, and replace them with affirmations of strength and determination. Earth to stay strong and grounded during times of withdrawal, weakness, or depression. Will also help you stay focused so that you can stay on the right path in your endeavors. Fire to protect yourself from relapse, and to burn away any influences that stand in your way. Will also help you take control over your addiction, or anything that stands in the way of success. Water to cleanse the emotions by washing away the desire that drives addictions. Will also wash away old grudges and emotional habits, leaving a clean slate for the road ahead.

Stones: Agate, black onyx, broken glass or earthenware, clear quartz, hematite, jasper, obsidian, peacock ore, tiger's eye.

Symbols: Broken chains, brooms, crosses, pentacles, suns, Xs.

CONFIDENCE AND SUCCESS

Mirrors: Inward to make the target shine brighter with good qualities, or make them see the best things about themselves. Outward to banish negative or unwanted habits, attitudes, and traits.

Colors: Red, yellow, white.

Herbs: Cane sugar, cayenne pepper, cinnamon, cinquefoil, lily, parsley, thyme, violet, white rose.

Day: Sunday, Monday, Tuesday.

Planet: Sun, Moon, Mars.

Moon Phase: New to full to welcome in new opportunities, search for jobs, and increase self-esteem and confidence. Full to help the target reach their full potential. Full to new to banish destructive habits or attitudes, and to banish other blocks that stand in the way of success.

Elements: Air for refreshing stagnant energies, helping one change their mental perspective to increase confidence, and helping the target believe that they're successful. Earth to help the target find stability, and to help them firmly stand their ground. Fire to ignite strength, self- confidence, and passion in their heart and mind to inspire them to go after what they desire. Water to help them love themselves unconditionally so that they can allow success to enter their life.

Stones: Amber, aventurine, garnet, jasper, moss agate, orange citrine, sunstone, tiger's eye, tourmaline, yellow topaz.

Symbols: Dollar signs, gold coins, gold pentacles, stars, suns.

ENDING A FRIENDSHIP OR RELATIONSHIP

Mirrors: This kind of spell is done with two boxes, both of which face outward (to passively banish two people from each other). Each member of the relationship is put in their own box. At the beginning of the spell, the boxes are set up against each other on the altar. Each day for the next moon cycle, the boxes are separated little by little until they're on opposite ends of the altar. For abusive relationships or friendships, you can use the mirrors in the same way as a banishing spell. Place the problem person in an inverted mirror box to send back their own evil, and put the victim in a box with mirrors that face out to protect them from their abusive partner until the relationship has ended for good.

Colors: Black, dark blue, dark red.

Herbs: Basil, black pepper, calamus, clove, dragon's blood, garlic, High John the Conqueror root, mugwort, myrrh, sage, yerba mate.

Day: Saturday.

Planet: Saturn.

Moon Phase: New to full to promote emotional and/or physical healing after the end of a relationship, and to help both parties move on to better things. Full to bring acceptance that the relationship has ended. Full to new to end a relationship, and bring passive separation between the people involved.

Elements: Air to help all parties come to terms with the fact that the relationship is over, and to promote mental healing after it has ended. Earth to keep erratic emotions grounded, and to reduce lashing out due to hurt feelings. Fire to protect those involved from backlash during or after the separation. Water to quench emotional storms, soothe broken hearts, and restore emotional balance in the lives of all involved.

Stones: Apache tears, black onyx, broken glass or earthenware, clear quartz, flint, hematite, lava stone, obsidian, red brick dust, red jasper, tiger's eye. Can also use any stone that has broken into two pieces.

Symbols: Brick or stone walls, broken hearts, knives, scissors, scythes, two boats sailing away from each other, unlinked or broken gold rings.

FRIENDSHIP

Mirrors: Inward to reflect off of the target good qualities that would attract new friends, or to strengthen existing friendships by bringing out the best in platonic relationships. Outward to banish negative habits that can sabotage friendships or drive people away, and also to banish any disloyal friends who are leeches and/or liars.

Colors: Brown, blue, pink, purple.

Herbs: Apple, basil, brown sugar, coffee beans, clove, lavender, myrtle, passionflower, pineapple, roses of any color, sage, yarrow.

Day: Thursday, Friday.

Planet: Jupiter, Venus.

Moon Phase: New to full to find new friends, or to help an existing friendship grow. Full to establish a new friendship, or help it reach its best potential. Full to new to sever an unwanted or stale friendship, or to banish problem "friends" from the target's life.

Elements: Air to call out to new friends, and to attract people who have similar interests as the target. Earth for stable friendships, to help find loyal friends, and to be able to stand one's ground during arguments. Fire to find people who share the same passions as the target, and to keep friendships exciting. Water to keep friendships from going stagnant, and to wash away hurt feelings when things are rough.

Stones: Amethyst, aventurine, garnet, hematite, jasper, lapis lazuli, moonstone, moss agate, peacock ore, peridot, rose quartz, tiger's eye.

Symbols: Cups, friendship bracelets, hands held together, intertwined circles, intertwined hearts, peace signs, stars, turtles.

HEALING

Mirrors: Inward to reflect good health back on the target, and to help heal sickness or wounds. Outward to banish existing illnesses, or to protect the target from getting sick or injured in the first place.

Colors: Light blue, white, yellow.

Herbs: Apple, bergamot, cayenne pepper, cinnamon, citrus fruits, elderberry, eucalyptus, ginger, lemon balm, mint, rosemary, sage, turmeric, vanilla bean, white roses.

Day: Sunday, Monday.

Planets: Sun, Moon.

Moon Phase: New to full to promote healing of any kind be it physical, mental, emotional, or spiritual. Even more abstract workings for healing — such as a broken relationship — can be done during this time. Full to bring diseases to their peak, and to realize the strength to get through them. This is also a good time to celebrate good health. Full to new to banish diseases or weakness, and to recuperate from being sick.

Elements: Air to heal mental diseases such as depression, anxiety, and nightmares. Earth to heal ailments of the body, and to help the target rest so that they can recuperate more quickly. Fire to heal a broken spirit, cure anger problems, or to heal someone who has lost their passion for something they love. Water to mend a broken heart, to help someone move on from a bad relationship, and to heal other emotional ailments.

Stones: Amethyst, azurite, clear quartz, emerald, garnet, jade, jasper, moonstone, moss agate, rose quartz, snowflake obsidian.

Symbols: Crescent moons, crosses, five or seven point stars, lilies, lotus flowers, Rod of Asclepius, spirals (clockwise to bring healing, or counter-clockwise to banish illness), suns.

<u>LOVE</u>

Mirrors: Inward for learning to love yourself, for helping you see that you're worthy of being loved, and for shining with your best qualities. Outward to banish negative habits and influences that keep you from finding love, or for protecting your relationships from being sabotaged (either by yourself or someone else).

Colors: Pink, purple, red, white.

Herbs: Adam and Eve root, apple (fruit or blossoms), basil, catnip, cayenne pepper (for sex magic), cinnamon, clove, cocoa/chocolate, dandelion, juniper berries, lavender, mint, rose, rosemary, strawberry, valerian, vanilla bean, yarrow.

Day: Friday.

Planet: Venus.

Moon Phase: New to full to make love grow. Full to bring a relationship to fruition. Full to new for a peaceful separation, or to banish an unwanted relationship.

Elements: Air to attract an intellectual partner who shares the same interests as the target, or to call out to a new lover. Earth for a stable relationship, and to be able to stand one's ground in any situation. Fire to ignite passion and sexual attraction, and to find someone who shares the same passion as the target. Water to keep a relationship from stagnating, and to cleanse a broken heart after a relationship has soured.

Stones: Clear quartz, diamond, jasper, moonstone, rose quartz, ruby.

Symbols: Ace of Hearts from a playing card deck (or Ace of Cups from the Tarot), cups/chalices, gold rings linked together, hearts, knots, pentacles (associated with the goddess Venus, and therefore the energy of love), rose pendants, turtle doves.

PEACE

Mirrors: Inward for inner reflection, and for finding the ability to forgive so that you can be at peace with yourself. Outward to banish the problem, which can allow peace by removing the disturbance altogether.

Colors: White.

Herbs: Cilantro, coriander, hyacinth (especially white), lavender, lily, sage, vervain/verbena, violet, white rose.

Day: Monday.

Planet: Moon.

Moon Phase: New to full to help peace grow between two people. Full to help you find peace within yourself after a difficult situation. Full to new to banish problems, remove the effects of arguments, and dispel negative forces to allow room for peace and quiet.

Elements: Air to help the target accept things they can't change so that they can find peace of mind. Earth to promote a down-to-earth approach to an unresolved situation, and to help one stand their ground while still allowing a resolution. Fire to help the target find strength within to forgive — but still remain strong — so that peace can be made. Water to soothe the emotional effects of a harmful situation so that the heart can find peace.

Stones: Amethyst, Apache tears, blue kyanite, clear quartz, flourite, moonstone, moss agate, opal, pearl, peridot, rose quartz.

Symbols: Doves, infinity symbol, olive branch, peace sign, white hearts, white flags, white roses, yin yang.

PERSONAL GROWTH AND EMPOWERMENT

Mirrors: Inward to open yourself to new experiences and knowledge that will lead to further growth. Also to instill more strength, and increase power through better knowledge of what you can do, and how to use it. Outward to ward off negative situations or thoughts that drain your power, or cause other setbacks in your spiritual growth.

Colors: Brown, green, purple, white.

Herbs: Apple, calamus, frankincense, High John the Conqueror root, lavender, lemon balm, oak, sage, watermelon.

Day: Monday, Wednesday, Friday.

Planet: Moon, Mercury, Venus.

Moon Phase: New to full to increase personal power, and to help you grow spiritually and mentally. Full to use what you have learned to its greatest potential, or to realize your greatest strength. Full to new to overcome setbacks and mental or spiritual blocks, and to banish influences that hold you back from advancing.

Elements: Air to open your mind to new experiences and information, and to help clear old thought patterns that hold you back. Earth to stay grounded, to help you grow physically stronger, and to develop and stick to a good work out plan. Also aids in using the body as a magickal tool. Fire to ignite personal power, and to crank up the heat so you can take your talents to the next level. Water to maintain balanced emotions so that erratic thoughts and actions won't create obstacles.

Stones: Amethyst, ametrine, azurite, black onyx, clear quartz, garnet, hematite, jade, jasper, moonstone, rare earth magnets, snowflake obsidian.

Symbols: Blooming flowers, clockwise spirals, closed fists, infinity symbol, lightning bolts, Nile River Goddess, oak trees, owls, pentacles, seven-point stars, suns, yin yang.

PROSPERITY AND ABUNDANCE

Mirrors: Inward to make the target reflect more luck and charisma, and to make them a magnet for money and new opportunities. Outward to banish poverty and bad spending habits, or to break free from a financial rut.

Colors: Gold, green, silver.

Herbs: Alfalfa, anise, basil, cinnamon, cinquefoil, clove, cumin, ginger, lavender, mint, orange, parsley, patchouli, pine needles, rosemary, sage, verbena.

Day: Wednesday.

Planet: Mercury.

Moon Phase: New to full to increase prosperity and opportunities. Full to bring new prospects to fruition, or help you reach your full potential and financial goals. Full to new to banish poverty, bad spending habits, and bad luck.

Elements: Air to help the target believe in their own prosperity, and that they deserve to have everything they've ever wanted. Earth to bring financial stability, and to make money grow. Fire to burn away blocks that are in the target's path to prosperity, and to ignite the passion inside them to earn big money. Water to cleanse their life of poverty, and to let money and new opportunities flow freely into their lives.

Stones: Aventurine, emerald, green jasper, hematite, jade, moss agate, orange citrine, rare earth magnets, tiger's eye.

Symbols: All-seeing eye, coins, cornucopia, dollar bills, dollar signs, fruit trees full of fruit, gold bars, horseshoes (pointing up), money trees, overflowing cups, pentacles.

PROTECTION

Mirrors: Mirror boxes for protection are usually made with the mirrors facing outward to deflect negative influences away from the target. However, they can be constructed with the mirrors facing inward to make the target's negative influence reflect back on them, which often has the side effect of driving the target away from the victim, or stopping the negative behavior altogether.

Colors: Black, blue.

Herbs: Anise, anything with thorns, basil, burrs, calamus, clove, coffee beans, dragon's blood, garlic, patchouli, rosemary, sage, stickers, thyme.

Day: Thursday, Saturday.

Planet: Jupiter, Saturn.

Moon Phase: New to full to create a protective force field around something or someone. Full for the strongest protection. Full to new to banish harmful people or influences, or to ward off negative activity.

Elements: Air to carry away harmful influences, and create invisible magickal force fields. Earth to provide cover for the victim. Fire to create magickal force fields, and to burn the attacker with their own evil. Water to wash away evil influences or energies.

Stones: Amethyst, clear quartz, hematite, red jasper, smoky quartz, tiger's eye.

Symbols: Brooms, crosses, eyes, hammers, hexagrams, pentacles, snakes, stars, Xs.

PSYCHIC POWERS AND DIVINATION

Mirrors: Inward to help the target sink deeply into their subconscious mind, and to help them get in touch with psychic powers hidden within. Outward to ward against psychic attacks, mind-reading, and harmful negative thoughts (the target's own or those of others).

Colors: Electric blue, electric green, purple, black.

Herbs: Bay, borage, cinnamon, dragon's blood, frankincense, lemon grass, mugwort, myrrh, nag champa, patchouli, sandalwood, wormwood, yarrow.

Day: Friday, Saturday.

Planet: Venus, Saturn.

Moon Phase: New to full to work on making psychic powers stronger, and to help find hidden answers to questions. A good time to communicate with the other side, and connect with lost ancestors and power animals. Full to take advantage of a peak in psychic power, perform the strongest séances, and carry out strong divination work. Full to new for inner reflection and meditation, and to do workings that ward off psychic attacks or negative thoughts.

Elements: Air to connect with the deep subconscious, to connect with the minds of others, and to open one's own mind to its inner psychic abilities. Earth to stay grounded and focused, and to sense problems with the body. Fire to connect with the spirit world (both the spirits of the living and dead, including one's own spirit). Water to connect with oneself and others on an emotional level.

Stones: Amethyst, ametrine, Apache tears, azurite, blue kyanite, emerald, flourite, moonstone, obsidian, smoky quartz.

Symbols: All-seeing eye, clockwise spirals, crescent moons, crystal balls, eyes, pyramids, stars.

TRUTH

Mirrors: Inward to make someone face the truth about themselves or a situation, or to make the truth reflect off of someone so that others know their true nature. Outward to stop gossip and slander, or to protect someone from another's lies (or their own).

Colors: Black, green, white, yellow.

Herbs: Adder's tongue, coffee beans, lemon (especially the seeds and thorns), lime, violet.

Ray Baker

Day: Wednesday, Sunday.

Planet: Mercury, Sun.

Moon Phase: New to Full to bring the truth to light. Full to completely expose a person's lies. Full to new to shut down gossip, or to banish a liar (and the effects of their lies).

Elements: Air to reveal the truth about a person or situation. Earth to help the honest stand their ground. Fire to burn a liar with their own dishonesty, or burn away their glamour over others. Water to wash away the negative effects of lies and gossip.

Stones: Black onyx, hematite, lapis lazuli, moonstone, peacock ore, smoky quartz, snowflake obsidian.

Symbols: Infinity symbol, justice scales, lemons, stars, the Ouroboros.

Sealing the Box

The last step to creating the perfect mirror box is to make sure you tightly seal the target inside. Doing so affirms that the spell has been completed, and isolates the personal effect so that the energies know exactly where to go. It's crucial to ensure that the box is completely sealed. One reason is that cracks left around the edges can let light and unwanted energies inside, which might have unwanted effects on the spell. The second, and more practical, reason is that a flimsy box will fall apart and break during handling.

I've found that plain invisible tape is the best way to close the mirror box. The tape seals the edges tightly, creates a sturdy finished product, and will contain most of the glass should the box break. It's also easy to remove with a razor blade or boline when the time comes to dismantle the box. Duct tape is another good choice, although it tends to leave a thick residue that's hard to remove if you plan on reusing the mirrors for another spell (the upside being that duct tape comes in a variety of colors that can be matched to fit the purpose of the working).

Candle wax also works great. Most of the spells in this book call for burning a candle of the appropriate color while carrying out the working. When the time comes to seal the box shut, I recommend taping all of the edges except for the lid (it's hard to get the first few mirrors to hold together with wax alone). Then, carefully drip wax from the burning candle around the lid to seal it in place. One time around should be sufficient, but depending on your tradition, you might make 3, 7, or another number of rounds while reciting your chant. Like tape, wax is fairly easy to peel off when it's time to open the box again.

Hot glue is another good option. It guarantees a good seal, and dries fast enough that you can make the box without having to sit for long periods of time holding the mirrors together. It's easy to peel away when you're done with the box, and leaves the mirrors clean for later use. When it comes to outward-facing boxes, I actually prefer hot glue over tape. It's less visible, and leaves more of the mirrors' surface area untouched. You can easily seal the tiles together on the inside of the box, then will only have to use hot glue on the outside for the lid. One downside to hot glue is that, like wax, it can be difficult to get the first few mirrors together. If you run into this problem, try using a little tape to get the first couple of mirrors started, then finish building the box with hot glue. I definitely don't suggest super glue, white glue, or any kind of epoxy. These are messy, take too much time to dry, and can stick your fingers together. They're also difficult — if not impossible — to get off the glass when you're ready to take the box apart. Try to stick to products that bond instantly, are easy to clean up, and are easy to remove from the mirrors without ruining them.

Once I've sealed the box, I sometimes draw symbols on either the lid or the sides. Symbols evoke certain images and feelings within our hearts and minds, which are then added to the working as we concentrate on drawing them. I usually drip symbols on with hot wax from a candle, or draw them on with a fine-tipped permanent marker. I've also done several spells where I drew symbols or verses on each of the mirrors before I sealed it shut, and visualized that the target was surrounded and overwhelmed by the symbols as they multiplied in the reflections.

The general meanings of symbols can be fairly universal (such as hearts, peace signs, and the yin yang), or they can be highly subjective depending on the experiences and cultural background of the observer. The pentacle is a prime example. Because Satanists have adopted the symbol, people who don't understand its origins see it as an icon of Satanism, black magick, and evil. People who have experience with the pentacle, however, know that it can represent anything from protection and strength to peace and love.

What matters most is that your chosen symbols represent the appropriate energies in your own heart and mind. Only use symbols that you're familiar with, and that have personal meaning to you. I usually use a pentacle for protection spells, a treskelion for return to sender workings, dollar signs for prosperity, hearts for love, turtles for friendship, et cetera. Palindrome spells, such as the SATOR Square, are another favorite of mine, and are easy to write on the mirrors. A friend of mine simply writes SMIB (an acronym for "so mote it be") on each side of the box to seal his spells. Use what speaks to you, or what you've come to know and love through your own experiences.

When you've finished a mirror box spell, it's important to keep the box somewhere safe so it can do its thing. Your altar is absolutely the best place for any kind of magickal item. However, not everyone's living situation allows them to keep an altar out in the open. If you have to hide your magickal items around the house, keep the box in a safe, inconspicuous place where you can still see it. When it grabs your attention, pick it up and shake it gently as you recite the verse from your spell (if the box contains heavy items, tap gently on the lid three times instead of shaking it).

If the spell deals with a particularly sticky situation, I like to designate a temporary altar or storage place just for the box. Again, this isn't mandatory, but I do feel that it helps keep outside energies from interfering with the spell. I made a separate altar for my spell to curse a thief since there were items the thieves had touched that wouldn't fit inside the box. I wanted these objects to be in contact with the mirrors, but remain separate from everything else in the house to avoid energetic contamination. I needed a magickally sterile working space, but also a power spot that would make me concentrate solely on that particular working while handling the box for the duration of the spell. Furthermore, I felt that the severity of the situation and the erratic nature of the energies involved warranted a designated space for the objects. In this case, I chose to put the altar next to the front door, where the thieves came in. Wherever you end up keeping the box, try to tend to it once a day — or at least a few times a week — until the time comes to close the spell. Doing so will keep the energies fresh, and keep the spell working strong while you wait for the results you want to see.

Tips on Writing and Casting Your Own Spells

Despite the fact that this book is geared toward practicing witches who already have a strong background in magick, I still want to give a few tips that I've picked up over the years on how to put together and cast a strong spell. When working with the mirror box, it can be hard to decide which way the mirrors should face, how the spell should be worded, and how to change existing spells to better fit your needs. Furthermore, no two witches practice in exactly the same way. Like anyone else, I have my own way of getting in touch with my spirituality, and some of my own methods for practicing magick. I would like to briefly share a few of the things that have come to work best for me, as well as a few topics that I approach differently than some of my magickal peers.

Since this isn't a witchcraft 101 book, I will not be giving beginner's instructions such as circle casting, calling the quarters, or performing invocations. My intended audience for this book is more advanced practitioners, so I assume that those using it are already adept at performing these tasks. I've also omitted these topics due to the fact that not all people who practice magick follow these steps as part of their spell-casting structure. I personally cast a circle and call the quarters before doing most spells. I also open my chakras, cleanse the area with incense or sage, and sometimes take a ritual shower before I begin my spellwork. If these things are part of your spell-casting ritual, then by all means feel free to integrate my spells into that format. If you're from a magickal tradition that doesn't practice these techniques, my hope is that my spells will mesh seamlessly with the structure you already have in place. I've tried to leave things as open as possible —without losing the integrity of the original spells — so that they will fit as many traditions as possible.

Another thing that some of my peers find strange is that, as a general rule, I usually don't use names of power in my spells. As an atheist, I don't believe that the old Pagan gods are actual conscious beings. I believe that they're simply personifications of certain energies, be they natural energies such as those associated with the weather, elements, and planets, or more human energies such as love, healing, protection, vengeance, et cetera. When I call these names out in a spell, it's simply to make a stronger connection with the energies that those names represent. However, I've never believed that I was talking to supernatural beings that come running at my command.

For example, where I used to call on the God or Goddess in my Wiccan days, I now say something along the lines of, "I invoke the great masculine/feminine creative energy which helped bring the universe into being." The same goes for the different gods or goddesses. Instead of calling on Venus/Aphrodite, I now say, "I open myself to the great energy that is Love. My mind, body, and spirit vibrate with the energy of Love. My circle is filled with the energy of Love." My goal is the same: to get in touch with the energy of Love so that I can use it in my working. The same images and emotions are evoked from within that would have been raised had I called out the names of spirits that supposedly reign over these same energies. In fact, I'm usually able to bring stronger images to mind by focusing on the energies themselves rather than on gods that are said to represent them.

I do, however, have an exception to this rule. Every now and then I will include a name of power in a working, but only when I feel that the name or image will help me get in touch more easily with their corresponding qualities. I often do this with spirits that hold a special place in my experiences as a witch — even if I don't believe that the spirit is an actual being. My "Santa Muerte Return to Sender Spell" is an excellent example. I fell in love with the image of la Santa Muerte through my studies of Spanish language and Latin American culture. Even though I don't believe that la Santa Muerte is a living spirit, I do have a certain affinity for her image and what it stands for. Using her name and likeness in that particular spell helped me make firm contact with what she represents, which helped me raise stronger energies to put toward the spell. In my opinion, this is the equivalent of using any other symbol to bring certain thoughts and emotions to mind. Some readers might not be willing to perform magick without names of power. As I said before, it's my hope that the spells I've given will fit comfortably into your existing system. If you feel that invoking gods or other spirits is vital to raising energy, then you should definitely do so when you cast.

Mirrors In or Mirrors Out?

Probably the hardest part of writing an original mirror box spell is deciding which way the mirrors should face. Many of the problems you might try to solve with the box will lie outside the realm of its two main uses (return to sender and protection). As you'll learn through experience, facing the mirrors in the appropriate direction can determine the success or failure of a spell. To keep the spell from backfiring, you must be sure the mirrors are facing the right way according to the goal of the working. You would normally face the mirrors inward for spells that send anything back to the target. This can of course be used for sending back negativity, but also for making someone take back hurtful things they've said or done, or for making someone keep their hands to themselves. Another use for the inverted mirrors is inner reflection; either to work through a tough problem, or to make someone see a situation they've been reluctant to face. Inverted mirrors can even be used to break creative ruts. I put myself in an inverted mirror box to cure my writer's block so that I could finish this book (the idea being to look deep inside my mind for the words that I was having trouble finding).

Interestingly, mirrors that are turned inward will not only reflect back people's true qualities, but will also make those qualities shine off of them with extra force. I realized this after the first few times I used the box in return to sender spells. Not only were my targets served a healthy dose of their own medicine, but also their true motives were drawn out of them like the head of a festering boil. Those around them saw them for who they really were, and began to shy away from the negative energy surrounding them. Seeing several of my targets succumb to these effects inspired me to use the box on people I didn't trust, which led to the development of the different truth spells you'll find in the next chapter. If someone in my inverted box was up to no good, the mirrors would draw the truth out into the open where no one could deny it.

On the other side of the spectrum, the same process can be used for self-improvement. Several of the spells in the next chapter cover how to use the inverted mirror box to make positive qualities more noticeable, and to help people find the confidence within themselves to put their best face forward. Many witches are firm believers that we attract that which we are. Using the mirror box in this fashion can help you attract money, success, confidence, and happiness by bringing those energies out in you to the point that they seem to shine off of you.

As for outward-facing mirrors, we've already discussed that this kind of box makes an excellent protection spell. It can protect the target from negative people, situations, and forces by creating a force field that blocks and banishes those influences. While many witches might use the box to banish an ex or protect themselves from harm, they could also use it to banish poverty, bad luck, depression, and many other negative energies that people struggle with on a daily basis. As with inverted mirror boxes, outward facing mirrors can be used to banish bad habits, or to become a better person by banishing the target's desire to continue certain patterns of undesirable behavior.

Additionally, you can use outward facing mirrors to protect assets that are rightfully yours. Chapter five will show you how to use the box to protect your house, car, and even your job by ensuring that other people stay off your turf. I've used the box more than once to protect my job when someone else was after it. I even walked in on three people breaking into my car after casting a protection spell over it, which resulted in those people being put in jail, and my property being returned to me.

These are only a few examples of what the mirror box can do, but will give you a good idea of how each kind of box works. The best way to determine which way the mirrors should face is to consider the desired result of the working, and then decide exactly what action you want the spell to take in order to reach it. Think about which way the energies should flow. Do you want to send energies back to or off of the target? Do you need to protect them by deflecting something away from them? You might want to make them shine with specific qualities so that others will see those traits in them. Or maybe you even want to force them to look inside themselves to face something they've been running from. Let your unique circumstances speak to you when writing original mirror box spells, or even rewriting the ones I've provided. Then, use your intuition and creativity to help you decide which way the mirrors should face when you build your box.

Wording the Spell: Say What You Want to Happen

The words are quite possibly the most iconic piece of any spell. When most people think of a witch casting a spell, they think of someone standing over a giant book, waving their hands, and reciting magick words that scrawl themselves across illuminated parchment pages. In some stories, havoc ensues if the witch recites a verse incorrectly, or accidentally leaves out a word or two. While this image isn't quite reality, it does show that even pop culture understands the importance of the verse to a spell.

Along with facing the mirrors the right way, it's important that the words to the spell match exactly what you want to happen. One of my biggest pet peeves involving magick is reading a chant or verse that has nothing to do with the working. I've read plenty of spells — some written by people who have been witches for over 40 years — that ramble on and on about the beauty of the Earth, the brilliance of the stars, and the pull of the moon on the ocean waves, but never even mention the purpose of the spell. Sometimes I just shake my head at a spell book and think, *I came here for a prosperity spell, not to read a poem by Robert Frost.*

Words aren't just mumbo-jumbo. Each word should be in the spell for a reason, and should tell the energies being raised what to do. Think of them as the script that the energies will follow once they've been released. A chant or verse might be the most beautiful piece of writing you've ever done, but if it has nothing to do with the purpose of the spell, then the energies will go on their happy way with no clear purpose to serve. Always stay focused on the task at hand, and be as clear as possible when stating what you want to happen.

Many practitioners think of the verses in spells as poems, and some won't settle for a verse that doesn't rhyme. I don't consider myself a poet, so I don't try extra hard to rhyme my verses. Nor do I usually make them extravagantly long, unless a specific spell calls for a longer verse. If you happen to be a good poet, then feel free to add that element to your spells. If not, don't be discouraged. Your workings will not be any more or less powerful if the verses don't rhyme, or don't sound like something out of a Shakespeare play. In fact, there is no requirement in poetry or spell writing that says the verses must rhyme. The most important thing is simply to say what you need to say in the appropriate time that it takes to say it.

Even though I don't focus much on rhyming my verses, I do try to give them a good rhythm that I can fall into while chanting. Many practitioners like to incorporate hand drums, rattles, or even electronic music into their chants to help them achieve the appropriate altered state of consciousness. A well-written spell will have a good rhythm that flows together with the music, and will help you fall into a trance while chanting. Even if you don't have music going, the verse itself should have some kind of beat that comes out as you chant it. The rhythm might not immediately reveal itself in spells that were written by others. Try to find your own beat in these cases, or at least a decent flow in the way you chant the words.

Finally, I would like to address spells written in other languages — mainly because I've included a spell or two written in Spanish in this book. While reciting a verse in another language can give your spells a mystical flair, you must always be sure you not only understand the spell word-for-word in your native language, but can also pronounce every word correctly. You never want to recite verses that you can't accurately translate, as you never know exactly what you're asking for.

Mispronouncing a word in a foreign language is just as bad. Sometimes slight differences in spelling or pronunciation will give two similar-looking words completely different meanings. A classic example comes from Spanish. The words *año* (ahn-yo) and *ano* (ahn-o) look similar, but the tilde over the n in *año* completely changes the pronunciation — and significance — of the word. Someone who doesn't have a solid understanding of Spanish might mispronounce *año* as *ano* in a chant, and end up petitioning the universe for a prosperous anus rather than a prosperous year (which, depending on your line of work, might still work out for you). For this reason, the spells that I've included in Spanish are immediately followed by their English translations. Still, just to be safe, those readers who are uncomfortable with their Spanish skills should stick to the English counterparts.

Raising Energy to Add Power to Your Spells

Raising energy during a working is another crucial part of casting a successful spell, and is what takes it to the next level. It's the difference between mixing mundane ingredients while reciting poems, and melding magickal energies that are bending to your will. Many advanced readers might think this is a no-brainer. However, I've been to several circles where the person in charge went through the actions of a spell and recited the verses, but failed to actually raise energy toward the working. If the energy in the circle is flat when you cast, you can expect the results of the spell to fall flat, too. While your spell might still work if you skip this step, I've found that spells that lack properly raised energy often give weak — if any — results.

Energy raising can be done in many ways, and is yet another aspect of the craft that everyone does a little bit differently. One of the easiest ways to raise energy is through meditation and trance. This involves inducing an altered state of consciousness where you can vividly visualize your goal as you fall into the rhythm of the verses that you're chanting. Getting lost in your meditation raises power in your mind, and then programs that power to perform the task you're visualizing.

Altered states of consciousness can range anywhere from "zoning out" or daydreaming to different levels of sleep. Some people are unsure how far under they need to be in order to effectively visualize and raise energy. The intensity of the altered state needed will vary from person to person, but can usually be achieved on the same level on which you can casually daydream. Those who are big daydreamers are already adept at falling into this state, and probably have no trouble raising energy through visualization and meditation. Those who are easily distracted by outside noises, or otherwise have trouble concentrating, might need to go a bit deeper (perhaps closer to a hypnotic state). With experimentation and practice, most people can quickly learn to effectively raise power in this manner.

Other practitioners use music and dance as their main technique for raising power. Drums, rattles, and flutes are commonly used in magick circles across many different traditions, and musicians are often a vital part of group rituals. They direct ritual dances, drive the rhythm of the working, and heighten the energies in the circle to astounding levels. Even when working alone, drumming or rattling is an excellent way to raise power during a working. Those who have trouble concentrating might find music especially helpful in inducing an altered state of consciousness. Pre-recorded music can even be used to help you get in touch with your subconscious mind, and provide a good rhythm to follow while chanting verses or dancing in your own circle. Repetitive drum music, chanting, and even modern day electronic music such as Trance and Dub Step all make excellent background music for raising energy.

Those who are familiar with the chakra centers know that they can be used to raise energy in the body. Opening the chakra centers through meditation allows the practitioner to tap into the energies that have been called into the circle. The body can then serve as a conduit to direct those energies at will. The seven main chakra centers run along the center of the body from the groin to the top of the head. The root chakra is usually associated with the color red, and is located just below the genital area. The sacral chakra sits between the genitals and the bellybutton, and usually takes the color orange. The solar plexus chakra, which is visualized as yellow, rests between the bellybutton and sternum. The green heart chakra is in the center of the chest. The throat chakra opens in the throat — where the Adam's apple sits in men — and carries the color blue. The third eye chakra rests above the eyebrows in the center of the forehead, and is thought of as deep indigo or violet. The crown chakra opens up at the top of the head. Depending on the tradition, it can be visualized as violet or white.

You can open the chakras from your head to your groin, or from the groin up. Whichever way you start, simply imagine a ball of appropriately colored light opening up in that area. While you visualize this, feel the ball of light spiraling open inside your body. Feel its energy pulsing within you as it charges up. As you open each chakra, imagine a string of light moving from one to the other so that they're all connected in your mind. Once all the centers are open, take a moment to feel the energy coursing through them, and then spreading out through your body and into your limbs. Practice directing this energy at will into your head, hands, and feet.

Whenever I open my chakras, I also like to open centers in the palms of my hands and the arches of my feet. You won't find these centers listed in every tradition, but they definitely exist, and play an important role in directing the energy you're raising. While the main chakras keep energy flowing through the trunk of your body, the centers in your feet let you draw energy up from the Earth, or discharge energy back into the ground. The centers in each hand also allow you to move and direct energy in and out of your body. For me, my dominant hand is the one that sends out energy, and my subordinate hand is the one that allows energy to enter my body. You can use all of these centers together to pull energy in, charge it, and then direct it back out during your workings.

These are some of my favorite ways to raise energy, and the ones that have always worked best for me. Different methods can — and oftentimes are — combined so that energy is raised on a physical, mental, and spiritual level all at once. As I said before, there are many more ways to raise energy, and the experience is a little bit different for everyone. No matter how you go about it, raising and directing energy into your spells is what ultimately breathes life into them, and will greatly increase the chances of them manifesting more quickly and accurately. Even in quick spells that you perform on the spot, taking the time to include some sort of energy raising technique will go a long way toward getting the results you want.

A Note on the Spells in This Book

Because the spells listed in the following chapters are all based on the same magickal tool, most of them will follow a similar pattern as far as their construction and execution. The major variables that will change from spell to spell will be the correspondences used, the way the mirrors face, the appropriate chants written to fit the purpose of each working, and other small details that might fit the overall theme of a particular spell. I realize that the spells might seem repetitive when reading them all back to back. Some spells evolved from earlier ones after they were rewritten to fit different situations. I wanted to include all of them to show how spells can be changed when need be, and how a few changes can make a major difference in a working. Each spell was written under distinct circumstances to solve a wide range of problems. Despite the fact that they all use the mirror box in a similar fashion, I feel that they show the versatility of the box, and how I was able to expand its two main uses into an entire network of spells. My hope is that my readers will use these spells as a foundation for writing their own, and that the mirror box will continue to inspire witches to turn to its power.

Mirrors In

As I discussed in the first chapter, the main function of the inverted mirror box is to reflect certain energies back on their source. Many times it's used to send back abuse, narcissism, or other behaviors that are affecting people in a harmful way. The following spells will cover those uses, but will also demonstrate that the inverted mirror box can be used for much more than magickal self-defense. From bringing out the truth when someone is lying, to making someone face their own reality, and even helping yourself shine with more self-confidence, the box can be integrated into almost any kind of spell. I've even used it to break creative ruts when I needed help getting projects going, and to make myself confront some of my own negative traits and fears so that I could work past them.

The inverted mirror box works much differently than one made of outward-facing mirrors. The nature of the box requires that the practitioner be extremely careful how they construct the spell, how their intentions charge the energies being raised, and how the spell is cast. Even when used to more positive ends – such as facing one's fears – the mirrors can bring the practitioner or target face-to-face with painful emotions that will need to be dealt with in order to move forward.

Another thing to consider is when it's appropriate to use the mirror box, and when another spell (or no spell at all) might be a better option.

Despite the fact that the mirror box is one of my favorite spells, I try to save its power for the right people and at the right times. If someone else is my target, I try to think about what they did and why, the other people their actions are affecting, and whether or not I might be overreacting out of anger or other strong emotions. Most importantly, I try to visualize what the outcome of the spell will be if I should decide to cast it. Over time, these ponderings have grown into a list of questions that I always run through to see if the mirror box is the appropriate solution for a given situation.

— Did they care about me when they did what they did?

— Did they care about anyone else's well-being other than their own?

— Do their actions warrant some kind of reaction (if I send back what they've put out, do they deserve what they get)?

— Do other people seem to have problems with this person, or is this something personal that I need to take some responsibility for?

— Do I have all the information I need to accurately assess the situation, and make an educated decision about what to do next?

— Did I have my own part to play in the way things have turned out?

— Am I extremely angry or jealous at the moment (do I need some time to calm down, and think things through)?

— Can this spell come back on me, or someone I care about, in any way?

— Am I willing to accept the consequences of casting this spell, no matter what they might be?

The first four questions deal with the moral code (or lack thereof) of the target. If my honest answers to these questions reveal that the target has no respect or empathy for others, then I usually have no problem using the mirror box on them. If my answers show that they are a decent person, but could be acting out of character in a certain situation, I might try a spell to bring peace instead, or maybe a working to get them to see their actions from the point of view of the people they're negatively affecting.

The next three questions have to do with my own point of view and emotions, and how those feelings could be negatively influencing my view of the target, or my view of the situation in general. There have been several times when being honest with myself about these three questions made me realize that I either needed more information before I could continue, or that I needed to step back and take a breather to avoid making the situation worse. Of course, there have been times when I've had to swallow my pride, accept my own part in the situation, and not cast at all.

The last two questions, in my opinion, are the most important on the list. I'm obviously doing something wrong if I feel like a spell might backfire on me for any reason. Along the same lines, if I'm not ready and willing to accept whatever consequences result from my actions of casting the spell, then I know that I have no business performing it in the first place. I will not use the mirror box when I feel the slightest amount of doubt concerning the last two questions on my list. In these cases, I sometimes go about things another way. Usually, however, I leave the situation alone for a while to see if it works itself out, or to see if a better solution presents itself at a later time.

The trick to success with the spells in this chapter is to be completely honest with yourself about your intentions, and about the culpability of your target. A quick run through of the list I've provided will give you more perspective on the situation, as well as on your own emotions, and how they might be interfering with your better judgment at the time. It's always better to play it safe with the mirror box, so only use it on negative people when they really have it coming, and when you're sure there will be no backlash on yourself or others.

Basic Return to Sender Spell

This is the spell that started it all, and the one that I originally overheard at the gathering more than a decade ago. I've used this basic spell to deal with the manager who tried to get me fired, coworkers who were causing me problems, and other less-than-desirable people who wouldn't stay off my back. This is the version that I usually recommend when someone is having problems with friends, exes, or even relatives who are trying to stir up trouble in their lives. Use this working as is, or as a template for designing and writing your own spells when the need arises.

Supplies: A black candle, an inverted mirror box, invisible tape, a photo of the target (or a slip of paper on which to write their name), your favorite crossing/return to sender herb or oil (I always use black pepper, lemon seeds, calamus, or basil), a black pen.

By the light of the black candle, begin by writing the name of the target on the back of the photo (or on the slip of paper) as you say in sets of three:

(person's name),
My words now bind
All the wrong you have done,
And all the negativity
You have sent against me.

Chant slowly so that you have time to go over their name several times, making the letters thick and dark. When you feel ready, hold your hands over the paper. Send your energy into it as you chant three times:

(person's name),
I place you in this hall of mirrors,
That all of your wrongdoings
And all of your negativity
Get caught in the reflections
That surround you.
That these actions be amplified,

Inside the Mirror Box

And turned against you,
To reflect back on you and off of you.

(person's name),
You are trapped now
In my hall of mirrors,
And these mirrors will show you
For who you really are.

Repeat the chant three more times while you fold the photo three times, and place it in the box. Sprinkle three pinches of your herb of choice (or three drops of oil) over the folded paper.

Tape the lid to the box. Drip the wax from the black candle over the lid in the shape of an upright pentagram. As you do so, continue chanting in sets of three:

(person's name),
You are trapped now
In my hall of mirrors,
And these mirrors will show you
For who you really are.

Keep the box on your altar, or in another safe place. Whenever it steals your attention, shake it gently, and repeat the last chant at least three times.

La Santa Muerte Return to Sender Spell

Once I started learning Spanish as a teenager, I found myself immersed not only in the language, but also in the vibrant cultures of the twenty-one Spanish-speaking countries of the world. I took a distinct liking to Mexican culture, whose Catholicism seemed to be less ashamed of its Pagan roots, and more open to the mysticism hidden in the religion. From Our Lady of Guadalupe to the early saints, the Pagan gods still reigned over celebrations such as Día de los Muertos and Candlemas. They showed an even stronger influence in actions such as burning devotional candles, and erecting altars to honor different saints. The more I learned, the more my spells became influenced by the magickal elements that my Pagan eyes saw peering out from the heavily Catholicized rituals and spirits.

One of the icons I fell most in love with was la Santa Muerte, or Holy Death. Although not an official saint in the Catholic Church, la Santa Muerte has nevertheless cultivated a massive underground following in Mexico, and in the Latino communities of the United States. Some images depict her as a skeletal version of Our Lady of Guadalupe. More traditionally, she appears as a feminine grim reaper with long, flowing robes that appear in different colors depending on the nature of the request being made. She usually holds a scythe in one hand, and a globe in the other. The scythe symbolizes many things, namely protection from negative influences, severing unnecessary ties, and the cutting of the life cord at death. The globe is said to symbolize the world in la Santa Muerte's hands, reminding us that we're all within her icy grasp.

La Santa Muerte might strike some as a Satanic spirit that people pray to in order to bring illness, bad luck, or death to their enemies. But upon further inspection, she's actually said to offer protection to the weak (especially those who face danger in their professions or daily lives), heal the sick, and perform other miracles. While the Catholic Church will not recognize her, she's still revered by her followers as a powerful folk saint with legitimate powers. Candles are burned in her honor for health and luck. Charms made in her image are carried by those who need protection. Her statues stand on altars decorated with offerings left by devotees in hopes that she'll grant them favors. Entire cults have sprung up in her name, and the number of followers increases daily.

I drew on the mythology of la Santa Muerte as inspiration for the next spell. It has the same effect on the target as a basic return to sender spell, but taps into the energies that la Santa Muerte represents to offer protection and support to those who are being mistreated. I first used it on a manager at a restaurant job who was sexually harassing and verbally abusing female employees. The women and young girls I worked with were subjected on a daily basis to screaming, profanity, and highly personal insults that would make any HR manager drop dead of a heart attack. Several of them had their jobs threatened after rejecting the manager's advances. One girl was actually fired for mysterious register shortages that showed up after she turned him down for a date.

Our boss, who acted much the same way, refused to hear any complaints (even when other male employees – including myself – spoke up about the situation). Complaints only led to typical excuses, and threats against our jobs. Worst of all, the owner's own behavior had created an environment in which the victims were afraid to file lawsuits for fear of retaliation outside of work. I became increasingly angry as I watched these things go on night after night, and watched our boss continue to let it happen. Since there seemed to be no mundane solution, I turned to my mirror box to help solve the problem.

After I did the spell, my manager started acting worse than ever. His insults were nastier, and he was going into hysterical fits at the slightest irritations. Customers were commenting on his behavior while they waited in line to pay. Things got so bad over the next week that two women went home in tears on the same night. I was starting to think that the box wasn't working, or that it had somehow backfired. What I realized later was that my manager simply couldn't handle the pressure of his actions coming back on him. His worsening behavior was the result of that pressure being put on him, and was setting off a string of events that would finally put an end to his abusive reign over the restaurant.

It started with the two women who went home in tears. Both of their husbands had been aware of the situation for some time, and were fed up with their wives being mistreated at work. After both men hit a dead end confronting the owner, they decided to take matters into their own hands. The first woman's husband showed up at the back door with a tire iron in hopes of catching the manager off guard at the end of the night. The other man caught up with him after work as he was pulling out of the parking lot, and ended up chasing him all the way across town in his truck.

Our boss wasn't happy when he heard about what happened. We were all hoping that, now that our manager's behavior was bringing violence right up to the door of the restaurant, the boss would be smart enough to get rid of him. We were wrong. While the manager did get into hot water for what happened on the property, he still didn't get fired. Nevertheless, I kept my faith in the spell strong. There had to be a way to make things better at work, and I knew the mirror box would find it.

The night the spell really kicked in was a particularly busy one for the business. We were all overwhelmed trying to accommodate the mass of customers flooding in, and our manager was in top form in the middle of a full-blown rage. During the busiest part of the rush, a customer asked to speak to the manager about the long wait for a table. His professional response was to pull the hostess away from helping another customer, and scream obscenities at her with a full audience of staff and customers. The lobby grew tense and silent as tears welled up in the girl's eyes. The manager stormed off, still screaming to himself as he disappeared back into the kitchen.

Several customers demanded to speak to the owner. One couple, after hearing that our boss had already gone home for the day, asked for a pen and paper. They wrote a detailed note about the manager's behavior, and asked that it be personally delivered to the boss. The cashier stapled the note closed around all three open edges. She then sealed it in the cash bag where the boss would find it when he counted the money the next morning. We all crossed our fingers, and hoped for the best.

Nothing was mentioned of the incident (or note) for several days. Then, the wife — who had written her phone number in the note— called to check in after not hearing from the owner. He was shocked to hear from her, as he didn't know anything about the note that she'd written. She explained the situation to my boss, and vowed to take her money elsewhere if the problem wasn't solved. She also threatened to spread the word online about how women were being treated there. After the owner reviewed the security video, he discovered that the manager had taken the note out of the cash bag, stuck it in his pocket, and later threw it in the trash. Not only had the manager lied to him, and stolen what the boss called "company property", but now the company's money and image were both at stake. The situation had finally become personal enough for the owner that he had no choice but to fire the manager.

As an atheist, I don't believe that the actual spirit of la Santa Muerte put her icy finger down to send my manager on his way. But I do believe that I was able to use the energy that she represents to fuel the spell. Considering the behavior of the owner, I knew I needed something stronger than the regular return to sender spell. I needed an energy that could offer protection to the victims while turning things around on my boss in a way that would make him understand the situation. La Santa Muerte helped me evoke these images while I did the spell, which I believe helped it turn out the way it did. Not only was my manager's behavior brought to my boss' attention in a way he couldn't ignore, but it was done so by people who wanted to defend the women who were being mistreated. The boss had no choice but to do the right thing once his money and image were put on the line.

The spell itself is a simple variation of the Basic Return to Sender Spell, but a few things will need to be gathered ahead of time. You'll need carnation or marigold petals, which are the two flowers associated with the dead in Latin America. These flowers are used to decorate altars dedicated to the dead, and sometimes appear in artwork depicting la Santa Muerte. You'll also need six small pictures of la Santa Muerte. A quick internet search will bring up plenty of options. Choose the picture that calls to you the most. Be sure to print it out small enough to fit in the center of each mirror, while leaving enough glass exposed to show a reflection. I copy and paste the picture into a photo-editing program so that I can adjust the size, and print all six copies on one page.

Supplies: A black candle, an inverted mirror box, invisible tape, six small pictures of La Santa Muerte, carnation or marigold petals, a slip of paper, a black pen.

By the light of the black candle, start by taping a small image of la Santa Muerte to the center of each mirror on the inside of the box. Feel yourself connecting with the energies of la Santa Muerte, and what she stands for. As you tape down each image say:

> *I invoke the energies of la Santa Muerte*
> *To aid me in this working.*
> *To aid me in turning back the evil*
> *That (person's name) has been sending out.*

Write the target's name on the slip of paper. Trace over it in thick, black letters as you say three times:

(person's name),
You will learn that
Your actions have consequences.
You will fall from grace
By your own wicked hand.

Repeat the chant three more times as you fold the paper three times, and place it in the box.

Sprinkle in three pinches of the marigold or carnation petals as you chant the verse three more times.

Hold your hands over the box, and pour your energy into it. Visualize la Santa Muerte's skeletal hands as your own, and fill the box with the power that spills down from your palms. As you charge the box, say nine times:

Holy Death,
Let (person's name)'s wrongdoings
Be reflected back on him/her.
Turn his/her misdeeds against him/her.
Let the innocent remain protected,
Hidden under the folds
Of your dark cloak,
Until justice has been brought down
Upon (person's name).

When you feel ready, seal the lid onto the box with the invisible tape. As you do so, repeat in sets of three:

(person's name),
You will learn that
Your actions have consequences.
You will fall from grace
By your own wicked hand.

Keep the box on your altar, or in another safe place. Each time it steals your attention, shake it gently as you repeat at least three times:

Holy Death,
Let (person's name)'s wrongdoings
Be reflected back on him/her.
Turn his/her misdeeds against him/her.
Let the innocent remain protected,
Hidden under the folds
Of your dark cloak,
Until justice has been brought down
Upon (person's name).

Cursing a Thief

This is one of my favorite mirror box spells to date. I wrote and performed it after my neighbor and I had our houses robbed at gunpoint by meth addicts. Thieves seem especially susceptible to return to sender spells, because of the connection that they have with the practitioner and their belongings. The Law of Contagion works triple time with thieves by turning everything they stole into a magnet for negative, self-sabotaging energies. These energies come at them in every direction, and stick to them like black slime. No matter what the thieves do, the energy that the stolen items carry will stay attached to them forever.

It starts with everything that the thieves touched and/or took. Once they lay their hands on something, they create a cosmic connection that can't be broken. Any money they stole — be it cash, credit cards, checks, et cetera — will be permanently attached to them as well. But it doesn't stop there. Anything they buy with the money they stole will carry the same negative energy that the money itself was charged with. Getting rid of the items they stole won't help, either, as any money they make from the things they took will also be cursed. Then, anything they buy with the money they make selling said items will be cursed. And the web will just get more and more intricate and tangled until everything comes crashing down on them.

The people who robbed me got to experience this for themselves. Less than a week after I did this spell, one of the people involved was pulled over by the police. My digital camera, checkbook, and part of my coin collection were all found in her vehicle, along with items that were taken from other houses the group had recently hit. Her house was then raided, which led to police finding almost $25,000 worth of stolen property from different robberies (and that was only what they hadn't had time to get rid of yet). They also found credit cards, bank accounts, and food stamp accounts that had all been opened in other peoples' names.

The property the police found gave them enough fingerprints and DNA to pinpoint the other members of the group. I'm not allowed to say more about the case at this time, due to the fact that it's still open and under investigation. What I can say is that Lady Justice still has her eye on the thieves. I've been keeping a spell going while I wait to hear back about going to trial. So far, the people who robbed our houses have had a lot of trouble staying out of jail. Their crimes are quickly catching up to them, and I'm confident that the mirror box is still working hard for me to make sure they stay behind bars.

So, how did I put the spell together that I feel brought the thieves out where the police could see them? I started by carefully going through the house, and finding small items that they had touched. They had rifled through everything in the house: my coins, drawers, papers, and closets. They had even ransacked my altars. This made it easy to find small items that would fit inside the box. Since the police ran forensics, I was able to use clear packing tape to pick up fingerprints in the dust left on different surfaces. (The thieves were kind enough to volunteer their own body bits, which are the most personal items they could leave behind for a crafty witch like me.)

Instead of my usual taper candle, I used a black jar candle that I bought from a small Mexican-Catholic shop in my neighborhood. These candles are good for stronger spells since they burn for several days, and keep the energy casting out for a longer period of time. I knew this spell was already working by the way the candle was acting as it burned. They usually burn clean and slow, with very little wax left on the sides, or in the bottom. During this spell, however, the candle put on quite a show. The flame stayed high, and burned extra hot. It changed colors between white, green, and blue the entire time it was burning. The wick stayed intact instead of breaking off, keeping the flame high so that it licked the edges of the jar. A thick layer of soot (what witches often refer to as lampblack) quickly formed on the glass.

What impressed me the most was that where these candles usually burn down completely, this one stopped evaporating two-thirds of the way from the top. The remaining candle turned into a waxy soup with streaks of molten black pigment churning through the inner clear wax. It burned several days longer than usual, then suddenly flashed out on its own. I had never seen a candle act quite like this one, and took it as a sign that the energy I sent out was definitely working strong and hard for me.

When performing this spell on any thief, try to get a body bit such as a fingerprint, or at least something that they touched while they were pilfering through your belongings. If you aren't able to find anything they touched, you can write a description of what was taken on a slip of paper. Throw this in the box with their name (if you know it), and the other items listed in the instructions for the spell.

Supplies: A black candle, an inverted mirror box, invisible tape, small items that the thieves touched (and/or a list of items that they stole), a body bit (if possible), a slip of paper, a black pen, black pepper, three dried lemon seeds.

Place the open mirror box in the center of your altar. By the light of the black candle, write on the slip of paper the name(s) of the people who stole from you. If you don't know their names, just write, "the person/people who robbed me." As you write, chant three times:

These thieves are bound,
Now, by my power.
Justice is served
In this witching hour.

Repeat the chant on each fold as you fold the paper three times. Toss the paper in the box.

Now add the items that they touched as you say three times:

I reach across the cosmic bond,
Which these thieves rendered
When placing their hands upon
The items once in my possession.
Bring them down by their own actions!

Add in three pinches of black pepper, and the three lemon seeds — one at a time — as you chant three times:

Every item that the thieves have touched
Is forever connected to them.
And every item that the thieves have stolen
Is forever connected to them.
And every cent that the thieves have stolen
Is forever connected to them.
And any profit that the thieves make
From the items they have stolen
Is forever connected to them.
And any item the thieves buy
With the money they have stolen
Is forever connected to them.
And any profit they make
From the items they have bought
With the money they have stolen
Is forever connected to them.
And through the Law of Contagion,
This spell follows that link back to them.
It hangs over their heads,
And it curses them
So that Justice has been brought down on them,
And they are made to pay
For what they have done.

Hold your hands over the box. Concentrate on sending your energy into it as you repeat the chant nine more times. While you chant, visualize whoever robbed you being arrested. See them standing, small and terrified, in court. Hear the judge's gavel bang. See their head(s) sag in shame. Hear the cell door slam as you see them thrown in a cold, dark prison cell.

Place the lid on the box when you feel ready. As you tape it shut, say on each side:

> *I close the box,*
> *And seal your fate.*
> *Lady Justice can no longer wait*
> *To get her anxious hands on you,*
> *And make you pay for all you do.*
> *The box I close,*
> *Your fate I seal.*
> *Justice comes without appeal.*

Drip the wax from the black candle in the shape of an inverted pentagram over the top of the box while you chant the last verse three more times.

Keep the box on your altar, or in another safe place. If your box contains heavy items, gently knock three times on the top each time it steals your attention. If it's light enough, you may shake it as you visualize the person/people who robbed you sitting alone in an empty jail cell.

This Is What Greed Gets You

Another spell you could use on a thief is the following working I wrote to turn back greed. The spell will turn their greedy tendencies against them in the same way the previous spell uses the items they've stolen against them. It can also be used on people who are obsessed with money, and always put their cash before their family or friends. Even if money isn't necessarily involved, this spell will help those who always put their own needs first realize that other people do exist.

The ingredients used in the working combine to create a simplified version of Hot Foot Powder. Commonly used in Voodoo traditions for banishing, it's said to put the fire under someone's feet to get them to scram. It can also be used for uncrossing, and to turn back negative energies of any kind. There are many variations, but almost every recipe calls for some kind of red chili pepper, black pepper, and graveyard dirt. I've also seen recipes that include gunpowder, black mustard seed, and sometimes calamus root. My simplified version is made from ingredients that are a little easier to find, but still works great for banishing or warding against unwanted people and forces.

Graveyard dirt is one of the key components to Hot Foot Powder. Although it can be purchased in many occult catalogs and online, I feel that it's best to take dirt from a cemetery in your town. Doing so ensures that you're getting authentic graveyard dirt, and not just sand out of someone's backyard. You also get to choose the grave that calls out to you the most. Personally, I'm always drawn to older graves that feel like they belong to someone who was important in life. You might be drawn to highly decorated graves, or a specific headstone might grab your attention. Some practitioners believe that ancestors who are sympathetic to your cause will actually draw you toward their grave, in essence giving you permission to take the dirt.

No matter which grave draws you in, you should always be respectful when harvesting the dirt. Read the name on the headstone aloud, and explain to that person why you're disturbing their resting place. Even if you don't believe that their spirit is present, go through the motions, and treat the plot as if it were your own property. Scrape the dirt from the top layer of soil, or from around the headstone to avoid leaving holes in the ground (you shouldn't need more than a handful or two of dirt, so this shouldn't be a problem).

When you have taken what you need, be sure to thank the person who's buried there. You might also have a small offering ready to leave behind. I like to leave a gold dollar, a piece of fruit, or a shot of rum. Fresh flowers or tobacco are also acceptable. Leaving the offering is not only out of thanks, but is a sign of respect for the dead. Since you're taking something from them — especially something that will be used in a greed spell — it's only appropriate that you leave something behind to replace it.

Supplies: A black candle, an inverted mirror box, invisible tape, The Tower card from your favorite Tarot deck, a dollar bill, nine red chili pods (or nine pinches of crushed red pepper), nine pinches of black pepper, nine pinches of graveyard dirt (or dirt from the footprint of your target), a slip of paper, a black pen.

By the light of the black candle, write your target's name on the paper in thick, black letters. As you do so, chant nine times:

> *(person's name),*
> *Your selfish ways*
> *Come back to bite you.*
> *Your greed and hunger*
> *Rise up to haunt you.*

Fold the paper three times, and place it in the mirror box. Stand the Tarot card behind the box so that you can see it clearly as you carry out the rest of the spell. Connect yourself with the energies that this card represents: in this case, the destruction of the inflated ego of the target, and the crumbling down of their false sense of entitlement. Concentrate on these qualities for a long moment, and see the target's greed bringing their world down around them.

When you're ready, begin chanting the following verse nine times. While you chant, tear up the dollar bill, and sprinkle the scraps into the box. Crush the pepper pods, and sprinkle them in with the dollar bill. Finally, add in nine pinches of black pepper, and nine pinches of graveyard dirt.

> *(person's name),*
> *You stand alone*
> *In this box of mirrors.*
> *With nothing in*
> *Your hands to hold.*
> *With no one there*
> *To stand beside you.*

As your little world
Topples down around you,
You find your only company
To be the words,
"This is what greed gets you."

This is what greed gets you.
This is what greed gets you.
This is what greed gets you.

Put as much emphasis as you can on the last three lines. Once you've added everything to the box, hold your hands over it, and pour in your energy as you continue to chant:

This is what greed gets you.
This is what greed gets you.
This is what greed gets you.

Charge the box with your energy for as long as you like. Then, continuing to chant, seal the box closed with the tape. Drip the candle wax over the lid in the shape of a pentagram. Keep the box on your altar, or in another safe place, with the Tarot card standing behind it. Shake the box any time it grabs your attention, and repeat in sets of three:

This is what greed gets you.
This is what greed gets you.
This is what greed gets you.

To Shut Down Gossip and Lies

Aside from return to sender, I've used the mirror box numerous times to expose the truth when people were being dishonest with me, or when a situation felt like it wasn't quite what it seemed to be. The next few spells show how the mirror box exposes a liar's true reflection, and casts them in their own light so that you can see what their hidden motives are. Whether your target is lying to you directly, gossiping behind your back, or trying to pull you into the middle of someone else's mess, magick can be used to expose the truth, and stop their activity dead in its tracks.

I first used the mirror box as a truth spell when an acquaintance pulled me into the middle of a fight that she started between a couple that lived on her street. A rumor that she was spreading out of jealousy quickly erupted into a full-blown soap opera complete with hair pulling, face scratching, and the boyfriend's property ending up in said acquaintance's front yard. Thanks to the rumors that were going around, several of our other friends also ended up getting mixed up in the situation. I still don't remember exactly how I got pulled into it (especially since I didn't even know some of the other people involved), but I did know who was behind the original piece of gossip, and I knew exactly how to keep it from going any farther.

I wrote the spell to send the rumors back to their source, and make the person responsible for them figuratively choke on her own words. Sure enough, my acquaintance's lies started catching up with her much faster than she could spin them. The people who were negatively affected started talking to each other instead of about each other. The tangled mass of rumors and exaggerations unraveled, and as it did, the cord that held it all together led right back to my friend who had started them. The mirrors shut down her gossip by reflecting back on her to expose her actions.

I originally wrote the spell in Spanish, which is my second language. If you understand and can comfortably pronounce the spell in Spanish, I feel that it would maintain its ambience in its original transcription. However, I've translated it into English for those who aren't familiar with Spanish, or feel they would be too distracted by it. I also want readers to be clear on the meaning of the spell, so that they know exactly what they're asking for when they cast it.

While I usually don't put absolute restrictions on moon phases or planetary hours, this spell taps into the energy of the full moon, and therefore should be cast at this time. Furthermore, the moon will start waning after you've cast the spell, which is the perfect time to remove the negative effects of gossip or lies, and to banish the person who's spreading them.

The full moon also shares some of the same associations with mirrors. For example, the moon's corresponding metal is silver (the same metal that was once widely used as the backing for mirrors). Some practitioners use round mirrors as a symbol for the moon in their workings. The moon itself could be considered a giant mirror in that it reflects the light of the sun back toward Earth.

One word of caution before you begin: you must make sure that you're not participating in the gossip being spread, and that the things going around are definitely not true. Otherwise, you're lying to yourself and others about the situation. You must have a clear conscience and a pure heart when casting this spell to keep it from coming back on you in unexpected ways.

Supplies: A black candle, an inverted mirror box, invisible tape, a picture of the person(s) causing you trouble (or a slip of paper on which to write their name), black pepper, High John the Conqueror oil (or another crossing oil of your choice), another slip of paper on which to write the chant, a black pen.

By the light of the black candle, write and say aloud the names of everyone who's speaking poorly about you on the backs of their pictures. If you don't have photos, simply write their names on a slip of paper. Say each name at least three times as you make the letters thick and dark.

Now say the following chant three times as you write it out on the second sheet of paper. You can use the Spanish or English version. You may also alternate between the two if you prefer.

A la luna llena y hermosa pido:
Se vuelva en contra
De estos hipócritas y mentirosos.
Póngalos en frente del espejo,
Para que enfrentarán a lo que han hecho.
Déjalos ahogar
En la mierda que hablan.

Beautiful full moon I ask:
Turn against

Inside the Mirror Box

These hypocrites and liars.
Place them before the mirror,
That they confront what they have done.
Let them choke
On the shit that they talk.

Say the chant three more times as you fold the photos (or slip of paper with the names on it) three times, and place it in the box.

Say the chant three more times as you fold the paper with the chant three times, and place it in the box.

Say the chant three more times as you put three drops of your crossing oil, and three pinches of black pepper in with the slips of paper.

Continue chanting in sets of three as you seal the box closed with the tape. Once sealed, drip the wax from the black candle over the lid in the form of a treskelion.

Keep the box on your altar, or in another safe place. Whenever it steals your attention, give it a gentle shake while you repeat the chant at least three times.

Let the Truth Be Seen Spell

The "Let the Truth Be Seen" spell combines the mirror box with another of my go-to magickal tools, which is the witch bottle. In traditional folk magick, witch bottles are said to trap curses or evil spirits sent out against someone, or to stop one person's harmful actions against another. Many times they're also used, much like a gris-gris bag, as a vessel in which to cast a spell. In this case a vial, jar, or glass bottle is filled with the ingredients and energies used during the spell, and then sealed tight until it has run its course.

I've used witch bottles by themselves for prosperity, to bring justice to someone who had broken into my car, to stop classmates from harassing me in high school, and to cool a friend down when her crush was unable to return her feelings. I've also used them, in conjunction with the mirror box, to get someone to tell the truth about a situation, or to reveal the true nature of their actions.

The first time I tried this was after the dream I mentioned in chapter two in which a friend was showing the contents of my flash drive to everyone at a party. As I said before, I try to listen to my dreams when they tell me that something isn't right, or that I might be missing something important. In real life, however, everything appeared normal concerning our friendship. I didn't want to start a confrontation over what might just be a weird dream. I needed to gather more information before I could decide what to do.

I started the mundane way by asking a few of our mutual friends if anything was going on or being said behind my back that I should know about. No one seemed to know anything at first. I then went right to the source, and asked my friend if there was anything that we needed to talk about. He assured me – with a big smile on his face – that nothing was wrong. Then, a short time later, another mutual friend of ours warned me that my friend wasn't who I thought he was. The dream, which was still in the back of my mind, started eating at me more and more. Still hesitant to start an argument over a dream and a vague rumor, I created the "Let the Truth Be Seen" spell to see if there really was anything to worry about.

Everything came out that weekend while I was hanging out with some of our other friends. As it turned out, he'd been showing strangers my Facebook page, and making fun of a project that I had been posting updates about each week. He'd also been starting conversations with me about our other friends in an attempt to get me to gossip about them, and was spreading rumors with them behind my back. What I found out is exactly what I was being warned about in my dream. The flash drive represented the sensitive information that he had at the tip of his fingers. Showing people the contents of the drive corresponded to him showing people my Facebook posts, and trying to get dirt on other people so that he could tell them what I said. Needless to say, I was disappointed to find out that he wasn't the friend I thought he was. But I was happy that the spell showed his true nature so that I could get him out of my life.

I used the same spell — with a different verse — to help a good friend come to terms with his cheating girlfriend. As I try to do in most cases, I attempted to talk things out with my friend before I resorted to magick. I let him know that I had been seeing his girlfriend going around with another guy, and that she'd been bragging about seeing him on the side. I even showed him several messages that she'd sent me online asking me to cover for her while she was with him, as well as the messages that I sent back warning her that I was going to tell her boyfriend what she was doing.

My friend admitted that I wasn't the first person to say something about what was going on behind his back. He finally confronted her, but quickly let her talk him into forgiving her. Meanwhile, the girlfriend, who thought it was hilarious that she was getting away with it, continued to parade the other guy in front of those of us who spoke up to her boyfriend. I knew my friend wanted to think the best of her, but I couldn't stand watching her toy with his emotions while blatantly taking advantage of him. Moreover, I wanted her to know that she wasn't going to keep getting away with it.

I actually ended up doing a different spell on each of them with two different goals in mind. I used the "Let the Truth Be Seen" spell on my friend to help him see for himself what was really going on with his girlfriend. Then, I wrote a spell called "The Brightest Star" to break the glamour that the girlfriend had over him, and to make everything she was doing shine off of her so brightly that no one could deny it. The spells, although they were doing different things, ended up working perfectly together. Not long after performing the workings, my friend finally came to his senses, and dumped the girlfriend like the hazardous waste bin that she was.

For both versions of the "Let the Truth Be Seen" spell you'll need to make a simple potion that I call my "Truth Telling Fluid". I've used this potion not only in the following spells, but also by anointing objects with which the target will come into contact. If the potion is fresh, you can even slip it into the suspected liar's food or drink. It may also be used to dress candles or amulets, or otherwise integrated into spells that seek the truth. Make this ahead of time, and have a bottle handy on the altar before you cast the spells.

Ray Baker

Truth Telling Fluid

<u>Supplies</u>: Dried and crushed lemon seeds, ½ cup fresh squeezed lemon juice, a silver or silver plated cup or bowl (if you can't find this, drop in a silver ring, dime, et cetera before you begin), an athame.

On your altar, pour the lemon juice into the silver cup or bowl. Use your athame to stir the lemon juice in a clockwise motion as you say three times:

I invoke the powers
Of Truth upon this potion.
All lies drop dead
Once its magick is in motion.
In its light all lies fade,
And break away.
The truth shines through
As clear as day.

Stir in three pinches of lemon seed, one pinch at a time, as you repeat the chant three more times.

Now hold your hands over the potion, and send your energy into it as you imagine it glowing bright with the light of truth. Do this for several minutes, or until you feel that the potion is adequately charged. With your index finger, trace a five-point star over the bowl to seal the energy.

Transfer the potion to a clean bottle or vial. Store it in the refrigerator for up to six weeks.

Note: If you have access to a lemon tree, you can use the thorns in conjunction with the potion. They can be added to your spell bottles, driven into candles, and even stabbed through a photo of the target. Use the thorns in sets of three or nine.

Inside the Mirror Box

Let the Truth Be Seen: Version One
(To Make Someone's True Intentions Known)

Supplies: A yellow or white candle, an inverted mirror box, invisible tape, Truth Telling Fluid, a small glass vial that will fit inside the box, a small slip of paper that will fit in the vial, a black pen.

Before lighting the candle, dress it with a few drops of the Truth Telling Fluid as you say three times:

(person's name),
I break through your lies.
I break down your disguise.
If you're lying and scheming about,
This spell will surely find you out.

By the light of the candle, write the target's name on the slip of paper. Trace their name several times, making the letters thick and dark, as you repeat the previous verse three more times.

Roll up the paper, and slide it into the vial. Fill the vial with the Truth Telling Fluid, and cap it tightly. Gently shake the vial as you chant nine times:

(person's name),
In this spell's light
All lies fade, and break away.
The truth shines through
As clear as day.
If you're lying and scheming about,
This spell with surely find you out.

Place the vial inside the mirror box. Carefully tape down the lid, saying on each side:

I seal your lies
Away with you.
The mirrors now
Reflect the truth.

Wet the tip of your index finger with a drop of the Truth Telling Fluid, then use it to trace an upright pentagram three times on the lid of the box.

Keep the box on your altar, or in another safe place. Since you can't shake the box with the vial inside, gently tap the lid each time it calls out to you, and repeat three times:

(person's name),
I break through your lies.
I break down your disguise.
If you're lying and scheming about,
This spell will surely find you out.

Let the Truth Be Seen: Version Two
(To Make One Person Accept the Truth About Another)

Supplies: A yellow or white candle, an inverted mirror box, invisible tape, Truth Telling Fluid, a small glass vial that will fit inside the box, a small slip of paper that will fit in the vial, a black pen.

Before lighting the candle, dress it with a few drops of the Truth Telling Fluid as you say three times:

(person's name),
I open your heart.
I open your eyes.
To the truth about
(other person's name)'s
Schemes and lies.

Inside the Mirror Box

By the light of the candle, write the target's name on the slip of paper. Trace their name several times, making the letters thick and dark, as you repeat the previous verse three more times.

Roll up the paper, and slide it into the vial. Fill the vial with the Truth Telling Fluid, and cap it tightly. Gently shake the vial as you chant the following verse nine times (say the other person's full name the first time you're required to use it. For the rest of the spell, use only their first name to maintain the rhythm of the chants):

(person's name),
You now see (other person's name)
For who and what he/she really is.
The truth surrounds you.
Shines bright in your face.
His/her lies unwind.
The glamour breaks.
Open your mind,
And let the mirrors reveal
The lies that (other person's name)
Tries hard to conceal.

Place the vial inside the mirror box. Carefully tape down the lid, saying on each side:

I seal (other person's name)'s lies
Away with you.
The mirrors now
Reflect the truth.

Wet the tip of your index finger with a drop of the Truth Telling Fluid, then use it to trace an upright pentagram three times on the lid of the box.

Keep the box on your altar, or in another safe place. Since you can't shake the box with the vial inside, gently tap the lid each time it calls out to you, and repeat three times:

(person's name),
I open your heart.
I open your eyes.
To the truth about
(other person's name) 's
Schemes and lies.

The Brightest Star Spell

This is another truth working that seeks to break down the power of a manipulative person in order to expose their true nature and motives. As the verse suggests, the mirror box reflects back all of the target's manipulations and lies, then makes them shine off of that person so strongly that no one can be fooled by their charms. They will be instantly recognizable for who they really are, and what they're really up to behind the scenes.

I wrote this spell for my friend's previously mentioned cheating girlfriend. It was one of the spells that helped my friend come to his senses, and realize what kind of person his girlfriend really was. A lot of her friends snapped out of it, too, and began to isolate themselves from her as the spell ran its course. Unfortunately for her, this resulted in winning herself a pretty ugly reputation. One that even her heightened powers of manipulation won't be able to repair any time soon.

Supplies: A silver or white candle, an inverted mirror box, invisible tape, a slip of paper, black and silver pens, a small piece of quartz crystal, 9 small reflective stars. (The stars can be made of cardstock that has been painted silver or covered in foil. You could also use small star stickers that have been placed on cardstock, and then cut out.)

By the light of the candle, call out the target's name nine times as you write it on the slip of paper. Trace over the letters multiple times, making them thick and dark as you repeat their name. Continue chanting in sets of nine as you use the silver pen to draw five-point stars around their name.

Inside the Mirror Box

Draw as many stars as you like, but make sure to fill in each one completely.

Fold the paper three times, and say on each fold:

(person's name),
You are the brightest, burning star.
Everyone now sees you
For what you really are.

Place their name inside the box.

Drop in the quartz crystal, and repeat the chant three more times.

Sprinkle in your silver stars, and repeat the chant three more times.

Hold your hands over the box, and send your energy into it. Imagine the box glowing so brightly that if it were actually emitting light, you wouldn't be able to look at it. As you do this, say nine times:

(person's name),
I place you in this hall of mirrors.
One looks back at you from the north.
One from the south.
One from the east.
One from the west.
One looks down on you from above.
One looks up at you from below.
All your manipulations,
All your lies,
Surround you,
And reflect back on you.
They shine off of you
Like the light from the brightest star.
Everyone now sees you
For what you really are.

Tape the box closed as you say four times (once as you tape each side):

I seal the box.
I seal your fate.
The truth shines through.
The glamour breaks.

Keep the box on your altar, or in another safe place. Each time you notice it sitting there, gently shake it while you say three times:

(person's name),
You are the brightest, burning star.
Everyone now sees you
For what you really are.

Let the Cracks Show Spell

Another spell that I wrote to show the truth about a person who's up to no good, this working helped me shatter through the façade of another good friend's cheating ex. The action of this spell works to break down the false image that others see of someone who seems like a great person, but secretly uses, lies to, or otherwise cheats other people. As the title suggests, the working will let the cracks show in that person's reputation so that the people around them begin to see them for who they really are. If they truly are up to no good, it won't take long for everything to come out in the broken reflections of the inverted mirror box.

For this working, you'll need to sacrifice one or two of the mirrors that you would normally use to build your mirror box. Buy an extra pack so that you have enough to work with. Try to choose mirrors that are already chipped or cracked, and save the good ones for the box. If you make a lot of mirror boxes like I do, you probably already have a few chipped mirrors set aside that didn't make the cut for previous spells.

Be sure you're wearing protective gloves before you place the mirrors in a small paper bag. Fold the bag around them, then lay them flat on the floor. With a hammer, gently tap the mirrors until you hear them break. Tap them several times so that you have pieces of different lengths and widths.

Carefully unfold the bag, and pour the shards of glass onto a sheet of old newspaper. Use tweezers to pick up the pieces of broken mirror, and strong, fast-drying glue to attach them —reflective side out — to each tile on the inside of an inverted mirror box. I recommend building the box first so that the pieces of glass won't be so close to the edges that they interfere with its construction. Also, when gluing pieces to the inside of the lid, be sure to leave enough room around the edges for the lid to fit properly at the end of the spell. Glue as many shards to the inside of the box as you like. The more cracks shown in the multitude of reflections, the better.

When the glue has dried thoroughly, the box will be ready to use in the spell. Take care while handling the box not to cut yourself on the shards of glass.

Supplies: A silver or black candle, an inverted mirror box that has been lined with shards of broken mirror, invisible tape, calamus root or crushed lemon seeds, a small piece of peacock ore, a small piece of spiky clear quartz, a photo of the target.

By the light of the candle, flip the photo of the target over, and write their name on the back in thick, dark letters. Call out their name in sets of three as you trace over it, and see their image clearly in your mind.

Turn the photo over, and hold your hands over it. Charge it with your energy, imagining in your mind that the energy is covering and soaking into your target. Say nine times:

> *(person's name),*
> *Your happy little life*
> *Isn't quite what it seems.*
> *No one else seems to notice*
> *How you lie and you scheme.*
> *With this witch's words,*
> *The cracks start to show.*
> *Doubled over on all sides,*

Then above, and below.
Your façade is shattered
Like the cracks that run through
The faces of these mirrors.
Now, show the real you!

Add three pinches of the calamus root or crushed lemon seeds, and chant nine times:

Let the cracks start to show.
Let the cracks start to show.
Doubled over on all sides,
Then above, and below.
The cracks in the mirrors
Reveal the truth.
The cracks in the mirrors
Reveal the real you!

Hold the peacock ore and the quartz in your hands. Charge them with your energy as you repeat the previous chant nine more times. Add the stones to the box.

Hold your hands over the box. Bring the image of your target back into your mind, but this time imagine that the image has been shattered, as if in a picture frame that has been dropped. Send your energy into the box, and repeat nine times:

(*person's name*),
Your happy little life
Isn't quite what it seems.
No one else seems to notice
How you lie and you scheme.
With this witch's words,
The cracks start to show.
Doubled over on all sides,
Then above, and below.

Inside the Mirror Box

Your façade is shattered
Like the cracks that run through
The faces of these mirrors.
Now, show the real you!

When you're ready, carefully seal the box closed with the invisible tape. Repeat on each side:

(person's name),
The cracks in the mirrors
Reveal the truth.
The cracks in the mirrors
Reveal the real you!

Keep the box on your altar, or in another safe place. When it steals your attention, or you find that the target is on your mind, gently shake it as you repeat the last chant nine times.

The Take a Look in the Mirror Spell

As the title implies, the next spell is for that person in your life who needs to take a long, hard look in the mirror. I originally wrote it for someone who was convinced that he could do no wrong, and liked to play the blame game when things weren't going his way. He never had money, because his friends wouldn't drive him around to find a job. He drank too much, because his friends made him go out every night of the week. Even losing his driver's license was because his friends didn't watch over him closely enough, and "allowed" him to drive drunk. Anything and everything that went wrong in his life was someone else's fault, and never his own.

His sense of entitlement, refusal to work, and denial of his own problems grew tiresome after a while. Everyone who cared about him wanted to see him do better. We still saw a good person who could get his life together if he would just change his perspective, and put in the effort needed to get himself back on track. But we couldn't get it through his head that he had to grow up, and take control over his own life and responsibilities.

While he never found out that I did it, my friend's stint in the mirror box did see some positive changes. He now has a steady job, has gotten his once excessive drinking habit under control, and is working on getting his driver's license reinstated. He has started to learn that many of his problems are his own, and that he must take responsibility for the consequences of his actions. Furthermore, his gradual change in perspective has led to him treating his friends with more respect. The good guy that we all knew was still there has come out of hiding, and will hopefully stick around for good.

You'll need the Truth Telling Fluid again when casting this spell. If you haven't already made it, refer back to the "Let the Truth Be Seen" spell for the recipe and instructions. While the "Take a Look in the Mirror" spell isn't exactly a working to break through lies or find out information, it does help someone see the truth about themselves so that they can face issues that they've been avoiding. Depending on the person you're dealing with, this will hopefully result in them being able to work past some of those problems so they can begin to make positive changes in their lives.

Supplies: A silver or white candle, an inverted mirror box, invisible tape, a square slip of paper (silver if you can find it), a black pen, Truth Telling Fluid, a piece of clear quartz, a piece of obsidian.

Begin by anointing the candle with a few drops of the Truth Telling Fluid. Work from the middle towards each end until you have gone all the way around the candle. As you work, see your target staring at their reflection in a mirror. See them examining every crease, every blemish, and every imperfection on their face.

Your problems are your own.
No one else can save you.
All will come to light
Once the mirror box surrounds you.

By the light of the candle, write the name of the person who needs a wake-up call on the slip of paper. Call their name aloud at least three times as you trace over it in thick, dark letters. Flip the paper over. Write a few words, as if you were writing directly to that person, explaining why they need to take a look at themselves, or how they're exhibiting self-destructive behavior.

Fold the paper three times. Say on each fold:

> *(person's name),*
> *You hold the power*
> *To create your own change.*
> *Open your eyes,*
> *And take the reins.*

Anoint each corner of the paper with the truth-telling fluid as you say three times:

> *(person's name),*
> *Look deep into these mirrors.*
> *Put your blame in the right place.*
> *Stare hard at your reflection.*
> *See what you need to face.*
> *Set aside your accusations,*
> *And let the truth arise.*
> *Let the answers to your problems*
> *Gaze back into your eyes.*

Wet the tip of your index finger with the Truth Telling Fluid. Use this to draw a pentagram over the paper. Fold the paper three times, and place it in the box.

Hold the obsidian and quartz in your hand. Charge the stones with your energy as you say three times:

Your problems are your own.
No one else can save you.
All will come to light
Once the mirror box surrounds you.

Add the stones to the box. Seal the lid closed with the tape as you repeat on each side:

(person's name),
Look deep into these mirrors.
Put your blame in the right place.
Stare hard at your reflection.
See what you need to face.
Set aside your accusations,
And let the truth arise.
Let the answers to your problems
Gaze back into your eyes.

Keep the box in a safe place. When it steals your attention, shake it gently, and repeat the chant at least three times.

The Wake Up and Smell the Coffee Spell

Like the "Take a Look in the Mirror" spell, this one was written to make someone realize that they're in control of their own choices. The idiomatic expression drives the intent of the working, as does the use of coffee as one of the correspondences. When the phrase "wake up and smell the coffee" is taken literally, it brings a solid visualization into the spell caster's mind that converts the words into a powerful symbol that drives the working. Furthermore, the aroma of the coffee perks up the senses, and therefore perks up the energies being fed into the spell. The caffeine can even be considered a spell activator that helps get things moving. Together, these correspondences create the perfect spell to grab someone's attention so they can snap out of a stubborn rut.

This spell can help the most stubborn of people see the real root of their problems so that they can begin to work through them. Students struggling in school, people in denial about their addictions or self-sabotaging habits, and those who might not realize how poorly they treat others are all good candidates. Even those who get taken advantage of by giving too much to people who don't deserve it can benefit from this spell. If you dare, you can even use the spell on yourself to gain a new perspective on issues that you're struggling with (I actually used this one on myself for that very reason). Whatever the problem, the spell will help the target see a situation for what it really is, especially if they're the cause of their own troubles. How they handle things from there is up to them.

Supplies: A black candle, an inverted mirror box, invisible tape, three pinches of unused coffee grounds or three espresso beans (if the target of the spell is a coffee drinker, try to get their favorite brand or flavor), a slip of paper, a black pen.

By the light of the black candle, write the person's name on the slip of paper. As you trace their name, making the letters thick and dark, say three times:

(person's name),
(person's name),
(person's name),
Your wake up call has arrived.
Wake up and smell the coffee.
It's time to rise and shine.

Fold the paper three times, and place it in the box. Sprinkle the coffee grounds over the paper, one pinch at a time (or add each coffee bean one at a time), as you say three times:

(person's name),
Wake up and smell the coffee.
It's time to rise and shine.
Pull the covers off your head,
And wipe the sleep, now,
From your eyes.

Your little dream is over.
It's time to face your life.
The cause of your own troubles
Shines in like morning light.

Hold your hands over the box. Concentrate on filling it with your energy as you chant the verse three more times.

Seal the box closed with the tape, saying on each side:

(person's name),
Your wake up call has arrived.
Wake up and smell the coffee.
It's time to rise and shine.

Drip the wax from the black candle in the shape of an upright pentagram over the lid of the box.

Keep the box on your altar, or in another safe place. Each time it calls out to you, shake it gently and repeat the chant three times.

Using the Mirror Box as a Glamour Spell

The next round of spells all work on a concept that witches call glamours. In magick, a glamour attempts to create an illusion that tricks the mind into seeing, hearing, or thinking something that isn't necessarily true, or to bring about qualities that are more attractive (i.e. glamorous). Many glamours have to do with beauty, such as spells that attempt to temporarily change a person's eye color, help them lose weight, cure skin problems, or improve other physical traits. Other glamour spells attempt to make changes to someone's behavior patterns or attitude so that they become a more attractive person from the inside out.

Glamours of this type are usually performed by the practitioner on themselves to help ease anxiety about their appearance or personality, thereby increasing their self-confidence. However, it's always acceptable for the practitioner to work a glamour spell for another person who needs a confidence boost. This can be in the form of casting a spell on them directly, or by using positive magick to touch them in small, uplifting ways.

For example, some of the witches in my community are fans of "glamour bombing". This consists of spreading good energy through random acts of kindness as well as through positive affirmations that are left where people will find them. One of my friends likes to buy rolls of dimes from the bank, and attach a star sticker to each coin. She leaves the dimes in parks, on bus stops, at the bases of trees, and along sidewalks. Not only is she spreading prosperous energy, but people will hopefully know that they were touched by a bit of magick when they see the star sticker. Other women in the group will write positive messages such as, "you are beautiful," "you have just been blessed by magick," "may your life be filled with healing, love, and prosperity," etc. They leave these slips of paper for strangers to find in hopes of bringing positive energy into their lives.

A more manipulative way to use glamour spells is to cause brief confusion, or to make someone fall under the impression that something is going on that isn't. If you've ever been the victim of a smooth talker, you know exactly how these spells work. Whether they realize it or not, manipulative people utilize the same tricks that witches do to create a glamour. They use their words and their will to make someone believe things are one way, when usually they're quite the opposite. This can be done to take advantage of others, to make someone bend to that person's will, or even to get out of some kind of trouble such as a traffic ticket or a reprimand at work.

Using glamours for these purposes definitely has its place, but should be approached with caution. Like any other form of magick, selfishly manipulating someone with glamours can have negative effects on the practitioner once the energy comes back to its source. Getting out of a traffic ticket is one thing, but tricking people into doing or thinking things that would normally go against their moral code will eventually harm all parties involved. Furthermore, glamours of this type don't last long. You might think you've gotten one over on your victim, but it will be easy for them to see right through you once the magick wears off. At the very least, they won't be able to trust you again. If they end up being a vengeful person, however, you may be in more trouble than you can glamour yourself out of later on down the road.

Self-inflicted negative glamours can be just as harmful. Sometimes people get carried away with negative thoughts and perceptions about themselves to the point that they actually start to believe them. These beliefs quickly take root in the subconscious mind, where they become bad habits and character traits. Anorexia is a classic example. People who struggle with anorexia have basically been glamoured — either by bullying from others, or through relentless negative perceptions of themselves — into believing that they're overweight, no matter how much weight they lose. Where outsiders might see a sufferer's body as skeletal and sickly, a person with anorexia sees a body covered in fat that they can't get rid of. Their body image has not only become an obsession that dominates their life, but also a negative glamour that has completely changed their reality, and the way they see their own body in the mirror.

Hypnosis works in a similar way. When you allow a hypnotherapist to put you under, they induce a deep meditative state in which they can tap into your subconscious mind. It's in this part of the brain that your habits, the ideas you hold about yourself, and all of your memories are stored. Hypnotherapists place positive affirmations and suggestions into your subconscious to help make permanent changes to your thought patterns. Depending on your goals, this could entail erasing the mental desire to smoke cigarettes, relieving anxiety by banishing emotions that are attached to past traumatic events, improving your memory, and so forth. The goal is to plant positive thoughts in the subconscious mind so that the brain will work to make those thoughts a reality in the person's waking life.

Much like hypnosis, glamour spells try to create specific changes by convincing the mind that those changes have already taken place. As you'll see in the following spells, the mirror box can serve as the catalyst for a glamour by reflecting positive attributes back onto or off of the target. Furthermore, it can be used to break negative thought patterns by removing them altogether, and replacing them with more positive affirmations that can raise a person's self-confidence, relieve anxiety, make them believe that they're successful, et cetera. The target of the spell will then begin to exude these qualities so that other people will begin to notice them as well.

Since the practitioner usually performs workings of this type on themselves, it should be made clear that placing yourself in an inverted mirror box can be a frightening experience. Part of instilling positive habits or traits is drawing out and eradicating the old, negative ones with which you've been stuck. The process can be emotionally taxing considering the fact that you'll be seeing yourself from the point of view of the outside world. You'll be putting yourself through a period of self-reflection that can bring up issues that are hard to face. The mirrors are never shy, so be prepared for them to be that friend that always tells it like it is, rather than how you want to hear it — even in a spell that works to evoke more positive traits from within. Placing yourself inside the mirror box truly is a journey, and it's one that you have to be prepared to take.

Moreover, it's important to keep your behavior in check while you're spending time inside the box. During the time that the mirrors have their attention turned on you, the way you treat others will come back on you more strongly and more quickly than usual. (If one of your problems is treating others poorly, this will be a good opportunity to really work on that part of your personality.) Conversely, if you're working extra hard to be a good person and treat others well, the mirrors will amplify your good deeds, and help others see those qualities shining off of you.

If you're worried about inverted mirror box spells coming back on you too harshly, chapter five will have ideas on how to use the outward facing mirror box in similar ways. While both approaches are effective, the outward facing mirrors will focus more on banishing your negative traits, rather than on bringing you face to face with them. You might start off with one of those spells to ease yourself into your self-transformation, and to give you a better idea of what to expect if you decide to try the inverted mirror box.

Spell to Make Yourself More Attractive or Loveable

The key to making yourself more attractive or loveable in the eyes of others is to first believe that you're attractive and loveable in your own eyes. The following glamour spell works to change your thought patterns about yourself so that the qualities you want others to see actually become a permanent part of your life. This particular spell concentrates on gaining inner beauty by changing your attitude about yourself, and emphasizing your positive traits to make them more noticeable.

Think for a moment about some of the people you know. Certain people seem to radiate with beauty and self-confidence, even if they might not use a lot of makeup, wear fancy clothes, or do their hair in any particularly special way. They get along well with others, and have little trouble making friends, or finding dates. These are the people who love themselves on the inside, and are confident not just about their looks, but about themselves in general. They treat others well, because they feel good about themselves. Other people see and feel the positive energy that surrounds them, and are naturally drawn to them due to their ability to spread that energy.

On the other hand, perfectly attractive people can easily make themselves ugly by the attitude they carry, or by the way they treat others. I've met several people who are physically beautiful, but tend to be avoided by others because they're either constantly putting themselves down, or carry a hateful attitude toward their peers. There are also people who know how attractive they are, and get carried away with their narcissism to the point that they become arrogant. Personality traits like these can be a huge turn off to others, no matter how nice someone is to look at.

There are, of course, many different shades on this spectrum. The point is that how you carry yourself, how you treat others, and your opinion of yourself can all have a huge impact on your image in the eyes of those around you. I wrote this spell for myself with the same concept in mind. I don't consider myself a physically unattractive person. Like anyone else, there are things that I would like to change about my appearance, but I know that my face doesn't clear a room when I walk through the door. I'm aware, however, that my attitude affects the way people see and approach me. My shyness, for example, makes it harder for me to start – or even jump into – a conversation with someone I don't really know. The result is that others sometimes see me as antisocial. I've even been told after meeting certain people that they were hesitant to approach me at first, because I looked like I didn't want to be bothered. I know it would be easier to meet new people if I had a friendlier demeanor, so "be more outgoing" was at the top of my list of qualities to work on.

Another big problem that I wanted to face is that I tend to be mistrusting of new people, which is another reason I seem antisocial at first. I have a bad habit of letting old problems interfere with new friendships, which makes me unfairly judge new people based on a lowered standard that I have of individuals that I've dealt with in the past. I've gotten into my fair share of heated arguments due to this lack of trust, and have caught myself overreacting when I think someone is being fake, or doing something otherwise backhanded. Therefore, "be more patient and understanding" ended up on my list, too.

I balanced the list out with a few things that I like about myself, but that needed extra emphasis so that other people would focus more on those aspects. Some of the things I wrote down were physical traits. Others were parts of my personality, and some were abilities that I think make me stand out from the crowd. I feel that this step is extremely important. Not only does it let others see the best in you, but it will also make you take time to concentrate on the reasons why you're already a good person who's worthy of love.

Sit down with a pen and paper before you cast this spell, and make your own list of positive qualities that you want to see more of in your life. Write in single words or short phrases, as you'll be transferring this list onto a slip of paper that, once folded, can fit easily inside the mirror box. It's important to be completely honest with yourself. Remember that this spell isn't designed to make you put yourself down, but rather to be honest with yourself about your strengths and weaknesses so that you can make positive changes in your life. The list will be sealed up tight where no one else can see it, so don't be shy about what you put on it. If you know you tend to be short with your friends, "patience" should be on the list. If you're painfully shy, "self-confidence" might be at the top of the page. Other things you write down could be, "beauty inside and out," "remember to love myself and others," "be friendlier," et cetera.

You should also write down existing positive qualities that you think need more attention. "Great cook," "beautiful eyes," or "romantic" are all good examples. Adding these things to the list will amplify them under the power of the mirror box, which will bring them out in you like never before. Especially if you're dealing with a tarnished reputation, placing more emphasis on your better qualities will show people your best side, which will hopefully influence them to forget about your past mistakes.

When you've finished your list, transfer it to the slip of paper that will go inside the box. Keep the paper in a safe place until you're ready to cast the spell.

Supplies: An inverted mirror box, a white or pink candle, invisible tape, your favorite essential oil (a scent that makes you feel good, and represents love to you), the list of qualities you prepared before the spell, a piece of rose quartz, seven rose petals, a small bowl of granulated sugar, a recent picture of yourself smiling (small enough to fit inside the box after being folded), a red pen.

By the light of the candle, use the red pen to write the following verse on the back of your picture:

My inner goodness and charm
Always shine through.
In the eyes of others,
And in my own eyes, too.
The mirrors only show
My best face to the crowd.
I stand strong.
I stand powerful.
I stand proud.

Turn the photo over, and hold your hands over it. See yourself smiling, and know that you're a charming person who's both loving and loveable. Send your energy into the photo as you repeat the verse seven times. Really emphasize the last three lines, and know in your mind that what you say is true.

Center the list of good qualities over the photo. Read each one aloud as part of the next chant. Repeat the process three times.

(positive quality),
Instill yourself in my heart.
Instill yourself in my mind.
Help me do better.
Make me shine.

Fold the photo and the list together three times, then place the package in the box.

Drop in the rose quartz, and repeat:

My inner goodness and charm
Always shine through.
In the eyes of others,
And in my own eyes, too.
The mirrors only show
My best face to the crowd.
I stand strong.
I stand powerful.
I stand proud.

Repeat this process with the rose petals, then again with three pinches of sugar, saying the chant as you add in each item.

Hold your hands over the box. Imagine that your mind is rearranging. That it's deleting your old habits, and replacing them with the new qualities on your list. Feel love for yourself rise up from within you, and send this energy into the box as you chant seven times:

Reflect deep into my heart.
Reflect deep into my mind.
Bring forth my finest traits,
And make them shine.
Under the mirrors' power,
The best me I exude.

Ray Baker

My vices are crushed
Under my best virtues.

Seal the box closed with the invisible tape, saying on each side:

The mirrors only show
My best face to the crowd.
I stand strong.
I stand powerful.
I stand proud.

Keep the box on your altar, or in another safe place. Shake it gently whenever it steals your attention, and know that your beauty is shining through.

Spell to Increase Confidence and Success

I talked in the last segment about making yourself more attractive and loveable by emphasizing your positive qualities, and making them stand out as part of your personal image. The next spell applies that same theory to confidence and success by helping the practitioner, or another target, believe that they can take on any situation that comes their way. Like the previous spell, this one works to glamour negative thought patterns out of the target's mind, and replace them with positive affirmations that promote higher self-confidence, and the ability to take action to reach specific goals. It calls on the power of the sun to help the target burn with confidence. That energy will continue to grow under the reflective power of the mirror box until the affirmations used in the spell become a permanent part of that person's psyche. Once they have the idea of confidence planted firmly in their mind, they'll be able to create their own success by boldly pursuing a new job or promotion, a college degree, a love interest that they've been too nervous to approach, or anything else they have in their sights.

Supplies: A yellow candle, an inverted mirror box, invisible tape, a yellow marker, a small picture of a bright sun, a favorite picture of yourself (make sure both the picture of yourself and the one of the sun can fit inside the box after being folded), the Sun card from your favorite Tarot deck, a small piece of sunstone, amber, or tiger's eye, cinnamon or white rose petals.

By the light of the yellow candle, write on the back of your photo with the yellow marker:

Shining sun,
Brilliant and bright,
Bring my confidence to light.
Cast your rays deep.
Help me find
The confident me
That shines inside.

Place your picture on the altar over the picture of the sun. Hold your hands over it, and feel your confidence welling up from inside you. Pour this energy out of your hands and into the photo. Concentrate on your smile as you say the verse you've written down seven times.

Place the picture of the sun over your photo, and fold them together three times. Add this to the box.

Stand the Tarot card behind the box. Concentrate on the image, and visualize yourself as being strong and self-assured. Your head is held high with a confident smile on your face. Know that you can handle any situation that comes your way, and that you have the strength and determination to make all of your dreams come true. Hold your hands over the box, and send this energy into it as you repeat seven times:

My will is the way
To all my desires.
My smile and charm
Never fail to acquire
Everything I want or need.

Confidence burns inside of me.
Nothing holds me back.
Nothing stands in my way.
I hold my head high.
I'm never afraid.
I stand proud for all to see
That confidence burns inside of me.

Add in the stone that you've chosen, and repeat seven times:

Confidence burns inside of me.

Add in the cinnamon or rose petals, and repeat the line seven more times.

Seal the box closed with the tape, repeating on each side:

My will is the way
To all my desires.
My smile and charm
Never fail to acquire
Everything I want or need.
Confidence burns inside of me.
Nothing holds me back.
Nothing stands in my way.
I hold my head high.
I'm never afraid.
I stand proud for all to see
That confidence burns inside of me.

Keep the box on your altar, or in another safe place. Shake it gently when it grabs your attention, and repeat the last verse seven times.

Spell to Help Face Your Fears

One of the biggest obstacles that people encounter each day is fear. Whether it's fear of embarrassment or failure, or an irrational phobia that takes over the body and mind, fear and anxiety can prevent people from living their lives to the fullest extent. From a primitive perspective, fear is a natural survivalist instinct that warns us when danger might be present, and helps us make decisions that could save our lives. A basic example is fear of snakes. Someone who's afraid of snakes will take steps to avoid them, which would hopefully prevent them from being bitten should they ever encounter one.

However, too much anxiety towards a particular thought or situation can develop into a phobia that interferes with one's daily life. Agoraphobics, for example, are known to experience crippling panic attacks in public situations. This oftentimes makes them avoid places like coffee shops, malls, concerts, and other locations where there are crowds of people. In an effort to avoid these situations, agoraphobics might not reach out to new friends, or even consider trying to form meaningful relationships.

In this way, fear and anxiety easily become another type of self-imposed negative glamour that places imaginary limits on the psyche. While it's necessary to be afraid of certain things, facing more irrational fears helps one overpower them, thereby reclaiming the parts of their life that have been lost to those fears. Magick can be used to force the target outside of their comfort zone so that they can break the hold that fear has over their mind, thereby enabling them to do and experience things that they wouldn't otherwise be able to do.

My fear-facing spell is another one that I wrote for myself to help me confront fears of my own. I was just about to start college when I first wrote it. I was a returning adult at the time, and hadn't set foot in a classroom in over seven years. I wasn't sure I remembered how to be a student, how to talk to other people in my classes, or even how to do a homework assignment. I was terrified that I was going to flunk out, and embarrass myself in front of my family, friends, and professors. I was afraid I wouldn't be able to work enough to pay my bills, or that I would even lose my job because of conflicts with classes. As that first day crept closer and closer, I found myself panicking like I never had before. I knew that things would get a lot easier once I made it through that first day. I just needed help getting past the enormous block of anxiety that stood in my way.

I chose the inverted mirror box because of its ability to make people face things that they don't want to see. I knew that putting myself in the mirror box was going to be rough, but I was determined to stare my fear in the face so that I could prove it wrong. Like throwing myself in a pit of hungry lions, I sealed my own name in the box with a large slip of paper that said, "COLLEGE." This simple symbolic action helped me find the strength I needed to face that first day (which ended up being completely monotonous, and nothing to be afraid of at all). I kept myself in the box for the entire first semester, which helped me get through the normal frustrations and uncertainties of being in a new environment with new people and responsibilities. It took some time to get settled in, but I was soon able to tackle any class I set foot in – even math (my weakest subject), and a two week crash course in 500-year-old Spanish literature that required reading a book a night in Spanish.

Facing my fear of college made me realize that I never had anything to be afraid of in the first place. College was definitely stressful, but it wasn't going to kill me. I wasn't going to flunk out as long as I did the work. My boss would just have to understand, and if he didn't, I could always go work for someone who did. I ended up graduating early with a 3.75 GPA, and can now be proud of myself for earning a college degree. Had I let my anxiety take over before I'd even given school a fair shot, I never would have been able to achieve everything that I did.

The fears that you're facing will obviously be different. You might be afraid of change, scared of public places, or might be stuck in a bad situation that you don't know how to escape. No matter what you're going through, the mirror box can help you take those first steps to confront your fears so that you can break the glamour that they have on you. Just remember that facing what you're afraid of will always cause some degree of anxiety. This is completely natural, so try to stick with the spell as long as you can. I kept myself in the mirror box for the remainder of my first semester, because I knew that the fear of failure and being new would keep coming back. Leaving myself in the box gave me the opportunity (and the strength) to continue facing those anxieties until they were permanently expelled from my mind. As the spell begins to work, take every encounter with your own fears as a chance to step outside of your comfort zone, and tackle them relentlessly. Keep reminding yourself that your fears aren't as big as you think they are, and that no matter what, you'll be O.K.

Before you make the box, sit down with a pen and paper. Write down what you're afraid of, and briefly describe why it bothers you. I recommend working through each fear one at a time to allow yourself time to process the stress and anxiety that comes with confronting them, but put as many things on the list as you think you can handle. When you're satisfied with your message, transfer it to a smaller slip of paper that will fit easily inside the mirror box. Keep this paper on your altar until you're ready to cast the spell.

Supplies: A white or yellow candle, an inverted mirror box, invisible tape, the slip of paper on which you have written your fear, the Strength card from the Tarot, calamus or High John the Conqueror root, a piece of hematite or peacock ore, a broken necklace chain that can be easily torn apart.

By the light of the candle, begin by placing the slip of paper in the center of the altar so that the writing is face up. Fix your eyes on the words that you've written. Imagine that those words actually are your fear, and that it's staring you in the face. Stare the words down, evoking all of your strength from within, as you say nine times:

I face my demons.
I stand strong before my fears.
I call on all my strength
To make these demons disappear.

Feel your strength rising up from inside you. Let it grow stronger and stronger as you chant. Know that facing your fear is as easy as staring at the words on the piece of paper. Know that just as you're able to do that without being harmed, you can stand up to your fear in real life without a second thought.

When you feel ready, take the slip of paper into your hands. Begin folding it into a tiny little square. Fold the paper again and again until it's so small that it can't be folded anymore. Each time you fold the paper, say:

> *Smaller, smaller, smaller,*
> *You shrink within my hands.*
> *What was once my biggest fear,*
> *Now smaller than a grain of sand.*

Say the verse at least nine times, then drop the paper in the box.

Add in three pinches of calamus or High John the Conqueror root, and say nine times:

> *I am bigger and stronger*
> *Than anything I fear.*
> *Demons, I command you:*
> *DISAPPEAR!*

Repeat this process with the hematite or peacock ore.

Take the broken necklace chain, and begin tearing it into nine small pieces. As you tear off each piece and throw it in the box, say:

> *I break the chains that bind me*
> *To everything I fear.*
> *I break the chains that bind me.*
> *I make my demons disappear.*

Stand the Strength card behind the box to remind you that you're stronger and more powerful than your fears. As you gaze at the card, let your strength again rise up from inside you. Send that powerful energy out of your hands, and into the box. Repeat nine times:

> *Smaller, smaller, smaller,*
> *You shrink within my hands.*

Inside the Mirror Box

What was once my biggest fear,
Now smaller than a grain of sand.
I face my demons.
I stand strong before my fears.
I call on all my strength
To make these demons disappear.

Seal the box closed with the tape. Repeat as you tape each side down:

I am bigger and stronger
Than anything I fear.
Demons, I command you:
DISAPPEAR!

Keep the box in a safe place. Shake the box gently whenever it grabs your attention.

Remember to take each confrontation with your fear as an opportunity to overpower it. If you need some extra help, close your eyes, take a deep breath, and repeat as many times as you need:

I am bigger and stronger
Than anything I fear.
Demons, I command you:
DISAPPEAR!

Should things get too stressful during the course of the spell, take the box apart for a couple weeks, and then try again. Do the same if your fear comes back after you've ended the working. Depending on how big your phobia is, you may need to start smaller, or it might take several cycles to find the courage you need to completely overcome it.

To End a Creative Rut

As a writer, I understand how hard it can be to come up with new ideas, or keep the momentum going on a project in which you've already invested a great deal of time and energy. It's not always easy to find the energy and inspiration to get those words on the page (even if you have a brilliant idea, a whole stack of notes, and know exactly what you want to say). This is especially true with larger projects that take a significant amount of time, motivation, and patience to stick with until the end.

The following spell came to me halfway through writing this book. I had two notebooks packed with spells and advice, a full outline, and plenty of outside resources. But I was running out of steam when it came to actually sitting down to flesh them out into a full book. I was also letting everyday life situations take me away from my writing. Picking up extra shifts at work, going out every night, and wasting too much time online were all burning the hours that I should've been spending writing. Before I knew it, I was eyes-deep in a creative rut that I didn't have the motivation to dig myself out of.

This spell helped me look inside myself for the drive and inspiration that I needed to keep myself going until the book was finished. I kept the box on my desk, and would place it right next to my hookah whenever it was time to write. I would light the hookah, and invoke the element of air before each session. If I got distracted, I would take a long hit of sweet tobacco, shake the box gently, and ask for inspiration to come from the East. Adding this to my writing ritual helped me relax, and made me stay focused on the task at hand. It also forced me to take a moment away from the word or sentence that was tripping me up, which is usually exactly what I needed to make things click back into place.

The working will function just as well for musicians, graphic artists, sculptors, actors, or any other creative mind that needs help getting in touch with their muse. Teachers and students can use the spell to get through lesson planning, grading, and the mountains of homework that tend to bury every student. In fact, anyone who exerts a great deal of mental energy in their line of work will find this spell useful. Even those who are in other kinds of ruts might rewrite the verses to fit their own unique situations.

For those of you who aren't hookah smokers, burning your favorite incense during your creative sessions will work just as well, and is what I've recommended in this version of the spell.

Inside the Mirror Box

<u>Supplies</u>: A purple candle, an inverted mirror box, invisible tape, a purple marker, a slip of paper, a small feather that will fit inside the box, your favorite incense (or a hookah loaded with your favorite sheesha mix).

Light the candle and incense in the name of inspiration. Close your eyes, and take a moment to enjoy the scent of the smoke as you take several deep, relaxing breaths.

While you take in the scent, open your third eye chakra by imagining an electric purple orb of energy spiraling open in the middle of your forehead. Feel the orb pulsing there, and let it grow incredibly bright in your mind's eye.

Face the east, and invite the element of Air into your sacred space by saying:

> *Element of Air,*
> *Keeper of the watchtower of the east,*
> *I call on thee.*
> *I invite you into this sacred space*
> *To aid me in this working.*
> *I invite you into this sacred space*
> *To witness this magickal rite.*
> *Bring inspiration into this temple.*
> *Let my muse find me here tonight.*

With the purple marker, write your full name on one side of the slip of paper. Then, flip it over, and write on the back:

> *As the mirror box*
> *Opens up before me,*
> *So, too, does my creative mind.*
> *New ideas and inspiration*
> *Stare back from every side.*

Hold your hands over the paper. Let your energy pulse into it while you repeat the verse eleven times.

Fold the paper three times, and drop it in the box. Place the feather in the palm of your dominant hand. Charge it with your energy while you say eleven times:

Light as a feather,
Floating on air,
Let my muse sing softly
Into my ear.
Bring new ideas.
Bring inspiration.
Break this rut
With motivation.

Let the feather drop slowly into the box. Hold your hands over it, and let your energy flow into it as you repeat eleven times:

I stare deep into these mirrors.
I look deeper and deeper inside
The vast, yet hidden dimension
That is my creative mind.
In this plane of reflections
My imagination opens wide.
New ideas and visions
Come into my mind.

Seal the box closed with the tape, saying on each side:

As the mirror box
Opens up before me,
So, too, does my creative mind.
New ideas and inspiration
Stare back from every side.

Inside the Mirror Box

Keep the box in or near your workspace. When you feel stuck on a project or idea, light your favorite incense, and invite the element of Air into your space. Gently shake the box, and repeat the last verse eleven times.

Compact Mirror Return to Sender Spell

Compact mirrors are a subtle way to kick back negative energy or shut down someone who's working against you. I've used them as a substitute for a mirror box when one wasn't available, but they also work great in emergency situations that require extreme discretion. They can be used at work, in the middle of class, and even in the car. Women can easily take advantage of this spell, as they might already have a compact in their purse, car, or desk at work. Men can keep a compact mirror in their glove compartment, desk drawer, with their magickal supplies, or in another inconspicuous location that will be easy to get to when the need arises.

Subtlety is the key to this spell, so keep it short and quiet. Try to excuse yourself to the restroom, your car, or another place where you'll be alone for a few minutes. Write the name of the person who's causing you trouble on a small slip of paper. If you have a compact that only has a mirror on one side, place the name so that it faces the glass. Visualize the face of your target in the surface of the mirror. Snap the compact shut, and say three times:

(person's name),
All you say, and all you do,
By the power of three,
Snaps back on you!

Hide the mirror in a secret place until the spell has run its course. If you need to boost it, tap on the compact case a few times, and say or think the verse three times. When you're done with the spell, dispose of the paper by tearing it up and throwing the pieces into the wind, or by flushing it down the toilet. Cleanse the compact in a salt bath for at least a week, and then save it to be used again at a later time.

Mirrors Out

In this chapter we will be turning the mirrors face-out, and exploring ways to use the outward-facing mirror box in even more spells. The outward-facing box hasn't been as popular in my personal practice as the inverted box, but it has still been an important part of my spellwork. Most practitioners employ it as a means of protection that isolates whatever is placed inside from harm. In magickal theory, the mirrors create a symbolic force field around the target (which is usually a person, but can also be a thing such as your house or car) that works to block and deflect negative forces. I've also found the outward-facing box useful for banishing negative people or qualities, breaking bad habits, bringing a peaceful end to soured relationships, and stopping unwanted advances or harassment.

You'll see in some of the following spells that there have been times when I've used the inverted and outward-facing mirror boxes together, or even two outward-facing boxes at the same time. The two can easily work in conjunction with one another to return negative energies to one target while protecting the other from their influence. Two outward-facing boxes can be used together to isolate two or more people from one another, or to create a gradual separation between them. Depending on the symbolism and intent of your own workings, you might even use three or four boxes turned different ways, or a smaller box inside of a larger one.

Like the first spell in chapter four, the basic protection spell in this chapter can be used as is, or it can be used as the foundation for creating spells of your own. Any of the other spells can be reworked to better fit your specific needs as they arise.

Basic Protection Spell

Supplies: A blue candle, an outward-facing mirror box, invisible tape, a photo of the target (or their name written on a slip of paper), basil, cloves, or rosemary; a piece of hematite, tiger's eye, or bloodstone.

Light the candle in the name of protection. Hold your hands over the photo or slip of paper. Push your energy into it while imagining the target of the spell surrounded by a pulsing, electric blue light. Chant the following verse seven times. Each time you say it, visualize the force field growing stronger and brighter. When you finish chanting, the person in your mind should no longer be visible through the barrier of electric light.

Thick like ice.
Hot as flame.
Protection, hear me
Call your name.
Surround (person's name)
From every direction.
Grant him/her your most
Powerful protection.
Give him/her firm ground
To stand upon.
Protect him/her from
All danger, sickness, and harm.
Any ill fortune
That could come his/her way,
Block it. Deflect it.
Send it away.

Turn the photo or paper over, and write on the back:

(person's name),
I cast a powerful,
Protective light all around you.
May it shine strong and bright
Wherever you go,
And whatever you do.

Repeat this verse seven times as you write it. Fold the picture three times, and drop it in the mirror box.

Add in three pinches of your chosen herb, and say:

Protective herb,
Breathe life into this spell.
Activate my protective force field.

Hold your chosen stone in your dominant hand. Charge it as you say:

(stone's name),
Give power to this spell.
Make it strong. Make it real.

Hold your hands over the box. Fill it with your energy as you repeat seven more times:

Thick like ice.
Hot as flame.
Protection, hear me
Call your name.
Surround (person's name)
From every direction.
Grant him/her your most
Powerful protection.
Give him/her firm ground

To stand upon.
Protect him/her from
All danger, sickness, and harm.
Any ill fortune
That could come his/her way,
Block it. Deflect it.
Send it away.

Seal the box with the tape, saying on each side:

(person's name),
I cast a powerful,
Protective light all around you.
May it shine strong and bright
Wherever you go,
And whatever you do.

Keep the box in a safe place, and shake it gently whenever you feel the need to recharge the spell.

Banishing Negative People or Influences

Another basic use for the outward-facing mirror box is to banish harmful people from the life of either the practitioner, or another target who needs protection. Where the first protection spell was more general in nature – working to grant protection from any and all danger – this version of the spell focuses on a specific person or situation that needs to be removed.

In the basic protection spell, a photo of the target is placed inside the outward-facing box, then the spell cast to symbolically build a force field around that person. This spell works in the same way as far as the person needing protection is concerned, but also places the person or situation needing banished beneath the box. The effect on them is similar to that of an inverted mirror box. They're not only deflected away from the person in need of protection, but their own influence is reflected back on them to help drive them away.

Supplies: A white candle, an outward-facing mirror box, invisible tape, a picture of the person giving you problems (or a slip of paper with the situation or influence you need to banish written on it), a favorite picture of yourself, a small piece of tiger's eye; basil, rosemary, or calamus root.

By the light of the white candle, write the following verse on the back of your photo:

Mirrors strong,
Mirrors bright,
Surround me in
Protective light.

Draw a pentagram or other protective symbol beneath the verse.

Turn the photo over, and hold your hands over it. Chant the verse seven more times as you charge the photo with the energy in your hands. See yourself surrounded on all sides, above, and below by outward-facing mirrors. See a bright light reflecting off of these mirrors that grows stronger and brighter as you chant. When you finish, the light should be so bright in your mind that it completely washes out your visualization.

When you feel ready, sprinkle in three pinches of your protective herb. Say:

With this herb,
The spell is sealed.
No evil can break through
My protective force field.

Hold the tiger's eye in your hands, and fill it with your energy while you say:

Tiger's eye,
Stand strong with me.

Ward off all drama
And negativity.

Place the tiger's eye in the box. Seal the box closed with the tape, saying on each side:

Mirrored walls,
Stand strong with me.
Ward off all drama
And negativity.

Place the box on the altar for now. Take the photo of the person needing banished (or slip of paper with the situation written on it), and set it in front of you. Concentrate on the person or problem as you charge the paper, and chant the following verse nine times:

Beneath me.
Below me.
Out of my way.
Don't even think
Of bothering me!
Try if you might.
Try everyday.
The mirrors will always
Turn you away.
Out of my reach.
Out of my sphere.
The mirrors make
You disappear!

Place the photo or paper, unfolded, in the center of the altar, then set the mirror box directly on top of it. Repeat the previous chant nine more times.

Whenever you feel like you need to boost the spell, pick the box up, and gently drop it down on the photo. Hold your hands over it, and repeat the last chant nine times.

SATOR Protection Spell

The SATOR Protection Spell uses an ancient palindrome charm as the catalyst for the action of the working. A palindrome is a word or phrase that reads the same forward and backward. Words of power that are palindromes are considered especially powerful in magick. The SATOR Square is probably the best known of these spells, and has been used by practitioners of various paths throughout the ages, including Christian Mystics, Pagans, and followers of the traditional Kabbalah. Most sources (including Walter O. Moeller's *The Mithraic Origin and the Meanings Of the Rotas-Sator Square*) agree that the earliest example of the charm to date was discovered in the ruins of Pompeii, and is one example of Paganism and Christianity blending together at a time when Christianity was taking over as the official religion of Rome.

The square is comprised of five Latin words that can be read in different directions. There is still much debate as to the exact meaning of the words used, but S.L. MacGregor Mathers gives one possible translation in his notes for the ancient grimoire *The Sacred Magic of Abramelin the Mage Book III* as, "The creator, slow moving, maintains his creations as vortices" (177). Alternatively, Godfrid Storms writes, "the sower shall keep the work of his hands" as another possible meaning in his work *Anglo Saxon Magic* (44). Similar translations have been given in other works studying the charm, but most point to the idea that the "sower" or "creator" shall be held responsible for its creation, and will keep things moving in proper order.

Because it spans so many traditions and has varying translations, the SATOR Square has become one of the oldest surviving and most versatile magickal formulas in modern magickal traditions. In ancient times, Roman soldiers carried the symbol with them for protection. In German folk magick, it was written on wood or a household plate, and then thrown into fires in hopes of extinguishing the flames. It has been displayed in homes for centuries to drive out spirits, protect the tenants and their belongings, and keep evil forces from entering the property. The charm has even found its way into popular novels such as John Updike's *The Witches of Eastwick*, in which one of the characters recites the words over a container of milk to transform it into cream.

Other palindrome spells have been recorded in grimoires and sacred texts throughout history. An excellent example is the aforementioned *The Sacred Magic of Abramelin the Mage*. This three-book sacred text gives palindrome spells and other magick squares for a wide variety of uses, and goes in-depth as to how to activate and use their power. The notes included by S.L. MacGregor Mathers give possible translations for the words used in the squares (many of which denote the action of the spell, while others are names of angels or demons that the square is attempting to invoke). Mathers also gives some information on the numerology behind the squares, which was an important part of their creation. The book is associated with both Christian Mysticism and the Jewish Kabbalah, and, therefore, does use different names from the Bible. However, many of the spells — especially the SATOR Square — have been used in magick of all traditions. Because of its age, the work is now in public domain. It can be found in a printer-friendly PDF format at http://hermetic.com/crowley/aa/abramelin1.pdf. This link will give you the first book of the entire work. Changing the end of the link to 2.pdf and 3.pdf will give you access to the remaining two books. I recommend printing them out, and keeping them in a three ring binder or your book of shadows as an invaluable reference material for your magickal studies.

Practitioners can, of course, create their own palindrome spells in any language that they can communicate in fluently. Those with a quick mind and the ability to play with words can easily design palindrome squares, crosses, or other configurations to fit the spells that they've written. Your palindromes don't necessarily have to be single words. Existing words can be combined, or letters can be rearranged to make new words that form new patterns. Numbers and musical notes can also be used to form palindromes, opening the door to a multi-layered spell that will be encoded with an intense amount of magickal energy.

To turn the mirror box into a palindrome spell, grab a ruler and an extra fine-tipped permanent marker. Be sure you're writing on the reflective side of the mirrors so that when you build the outward-facing box, the charm will be on the outside. For a SATOR Square, you'll need to divide each mirror into a 5 x 5 grid with a total of 25 squares. Unless you're using a 5'' square mirror, your ruler will probably not have hatch marks that will equally divide the mirrors into fifths. The grid doesn't have to be perfect, so you can estimate to make the rows as even as possible. I like to make small tick marks all the way around the mirror where each line needs to be, and then use the edge of the ruler to connect the lines so that they're nice and straight. Repeat this process with each mirror, but don't write in the SATOR Square, and don't build the box. Both of these actions will be done during the spell so that they can be charged as part of the working.

Supplies: A blue or white candle, six mirrors with 5 x 5 grids drawn on them, invisible tape, a photo of the target, a fine-tipped permanent marker, seven pinches of dried rosemary and sage, a small piece of clear quartz.

By the light of the candle, use the fine-tipped marker to begin filling in the SATOR Square on each mirror. Call out each word as you write it on the glass, so that you have chanted the palindrome once for each mirror:

SATOR
AREPO
TENET
OPERA
ROTAS

When you've completed that step, spread the mirrors out — reflective side up — on the altar. Hold your hands over them, and begin to charge them with your energy. Imagine the glass glowing with a bright, pulsing white light as you chant seven times:

I invoke the power
Of this ancient charm
To protect (person's name)
From ill will and harm.
Forward,

Backward,
Below and above.
Surround (person's name)
With protection and love.
No danger can pass
Through this sacred square.
Evil is driven away
By its own face in the mirror.

Build the mirror box as you normally would, leaving the lid off so that you can add the rest of the components for the spell. Take care not to rub off the letters that you've written on the glass as you build the box. If any of the letters do get removed, touch them back up before continuing the spell.

Turn the photo of the target face down, and write the SATOR Square on the back of the photo with the marker. Flip it back over, and hold your hands over it. Send your energy into the photo, imagining the target glowing with a bright, protective light as you repeat the previous verse seven more times. When you feel ready, fold the picture three times, and place it in the box.

Add in seven pinches of the rosemary and sage leaves, saying as you add each pinch:

Protective herb,
Breathe life into this spell.
Activate my protective force field.

Hold the quartz crystal in your hands. Send your energy into it as you say seven times:

Sacred stone
Of Earth and Fire,
Ignite this spell's
Protective power.

Add the stone to the box. Hold your hands over it, and let your energy flow down into it. Visualize the box glowing with a bright, protective light as you repeat seven more times:

I invoke the power
Of this ancient charm
To protect (person's name)
From ill will and harm.
Forward,
Backward,
Below and above.
Surround (person's name)
With protection and love.
No danger can pass
Through this sacred square.
Evil is driven away
By its own face in the mirror.

Seal the lid on the box with the invisible tape. As you tape down each side, repeat the SATOR charm:

SATOR
AREPO
TENET
OPERA
ROTAS

Keep the box on your altar, or in another safe place. When you feel like you need extra protection, gently shake the box while you repeat the SATOR charm seven times.

Using the Mirror Box to Protect Your Assets

In addition to protecting yourself or others, the outward-facing mirror box can be employed in spells to cast protection around your assets. This can include physical objects such as your car, house, or other property, or more intangible things like your finances or relationship. I first used the box in this way to cast a protection spell over my car after an increase in car thefts and break-ins in my neighborhood. The make and model of my vehicle at the time was a prime target for theft since it was easy to push-start, and the parts were in high demand. Thieves in my town were getting increasingly confident, too, going so far as to steal cars out of parking lots in broad daylight. Since my vehicle was on the most wanted list, I figured the mirror box would be a great way to make sure my vehicle was protected from theft and other damage.

Just days after building the mirror box, I walked out of a store to find three people rifling through my car – one at each door, and one in the trunk. They had jimmied down my window while I was inside, and were scrambling to find anything they could get their hands on (which wasn't much, since I never leave valuables in the car in the first place). I immediately called the police, which the thieves noticed once they heard me yelling into my cell phone. They dropped the few things that they had grabbed (they were seriously so desperate that they tried to make off with my car jack, spare tire, and a few badly scratched CDs that I had forgotten in the glove box), and jumped in the vehicle they were driving. The driver backed out all the way across the parking lot, hoping that I wouldn't see the license plate. Still, I was able to catch the first few letters, which was enough for the police to identify the tag a few blocks down the street.

The thieves were pulled over before I even hung up with dispatch, and all three of them were arrested. My car was unharmed, and all of my property made it back to me. I was surprised at how quickly the police were able to act in that particular situation. It was as if they had been called to that area of town just in time for the incident to unfold. What really made me smile was that the thieves still had their trunk loaded to the top with purses, backpacks, car stereos, and other property that they had been pilfering all week long. Many of the other victims were able to get their belongings back thanks, from my perception, to the protection spell that I put on my vehicle.

The following spells will add some protective magick not only to your car, but also to your house, job, and relationship. The spell to protect the home can be rewritten for use by business owners, or to protect other buildings such as a shed, garage, barn, et cetera. Like other mirror box spells, the contents and chants will change to fit the specific need of the working. Use these next few examples as a guideline to write protection spells for other assets that are important to you.

I've noticed with this set of spells that they need to be recharged often to maintain their strength. Shaking the box on a regular basis will help keep energy flowing into the workings, but I do recommend repeating them once every two or three months for maximum effect.

To Protect Your Car

Supplies: A blue candle, an outward-facing mirror box, invisible tape, seven cloves or seven rosemary leaves, a small piece of tiger's eye, one of the following: a picture of your car, a small toy car that will fit inside the box, or a slip of paper with the color, make, model, year, and plate number written on it.

By the light of the blue candle, hold the item that represents your car in your hands. Send your energy into it as you visualize a bright, electric blue bubble forming around the vehicle. Let the bubble grow strong and bright in your mind while you chant seven times:

I cast a protective circle
Around my loyal vehicle.
Within, without,
From wheel to wheel,
Protection solid,
And strong as steel.

Add the item to the mirror box (if using a photo or slip of paper, fold it three times before adding it).

Sprinkle in the cloves or rosemary as you say:

Sacred herb,
Breathe life into my spell.
Activate my protective force field.

Drop in the tiger's eye, and say:

Enforced and reinforced
Is the protective force
That surrounds my car.
Protection come,
From near and far.

Hold your hands over the box. Let your energy flow into it as you bring back your visualization of the protective bubble around your vehicle. Imagine the blue light becoming thick and solid until it creates an impenetrable barrier around your car. As you visualize this, say seven times:

Thick like ice, and hard as steel.
Mirrors make a magick force field.
Make my car invisible to thieves.
Avoid all wrecks, marks, and dings.
Whether parked, in gear, or driving around,
No damage or thieves anywhere to be found.
Within, without, from wheel to wheel,
Protection solid, and strong as steel.

When you feel ready, seal the box closed with the tape. You can keep it on your altar, or in an inconspicuous place in the car where it won't get broken or handled by others. Every now and then, gently shake the box to recharge it (if you used a heavy toy car, tap on the lid instead). Repeat seven times:

Within, without,
From wheel to wheel,
Protection solid,
And strong as steel.

Inside the Mirror Box

To Protect Your Home

Supplies: A blue candle, an outward-facing mirror box, invisible tape, a piece of rose quartz, a piece of clear quartz, seven anise seeds or seven cloves, and one of the following: a photo of your house/apartment building, a plastic toy house, or your address written on a slip of paper.

By the light of the blue candle, hold the item that represents your home in your hands. Send your energy into it as you visualize a bright, blue circle forming around the property. See the circle getting brighter and thicker until you can no longer see the building through its barrier. As you do so, say seven times:

> *I cast a protective circle*
> *Around the barriers*
> *Of my property.*
> *It glows bright and impenetrable,*
> *Powerful and unfaltering.*
> *Nothing harmful can cross*
> *My magick force field.*
> *Any evil that comes near*
> *Will turn, running, on its heel.*

Add the representation of your home to the box (if using a photo or slip of paper, fold it three times before adding it).

Sprinkle in the anise seeds or cloves as you say:

> *Sacred herb,*
> *Breathe life into my spell.*
> *Activate my protective force field.*

Hold both of the quartz crystals in your hands. Let your energy pulse into them as you say:

Ancient quartz
Of Earth and Fire,
Empower this spell.
Manifest my desire.
Our powers meld,
And intertwine.
Cast protection
Over what is mine.

Add the stones to the box. Hold your hands over it, and gently pour your energy into it. Begin to chant the next verse seven times. As you do so, follow the imagery of the verse, and imagine a giant mirror springing up from the ground around each side of the force field that you have already created in your mind. Then imagine a giant mirror coming down from the sky, and another one up from the ground, so that an outward-facing mirror box is formed around the property in your mind's eye.

Protection,
I summon you from the North.
I call you forth from the South.
Come, now, from the West.
And from the East,
Without a doubt.
Come down from above,
And also up from down below.
Surround this property.
Protect my home.
Reflect, deflect,
And send away
All thieves and negativity.
Protect this home.
Keep storms at bay.
Deflect all harm
That might come this way.

When you feel ready, seal the lid onto the box with the tape while saying on each side:

> *I seal this spell*
> *Once and for all.*
> *My protective walls*
> *Will never fall.*

Keep it on your altar, or in another safe place in the home. When you feel like you need a little extra protection, shake the box gently while you say seven times:

> *I cast a protective circle*
> *Around the barriers*
> *Of my property.*
> *It glows bright and impenetrable,*
> *Powerful and unfaltering.*
> *Nothing harmful can cross*
> *My magick force field.*
> *Any evil that comes near*
> *Will turn, running, on its heel.*

To Protect Your Job

Supplies: A blue candle, an outward-facing mirror box, invisible tape, a picture of yourself, a slip of paper with the name of your workplace written on it, a picture of the person giving you problems at work (or their name written on a slip of paper), one of the following: dragon's blood herb, calamus root, or seven cloves.

By the light of the candle, write the following verse on the back of your photo:

> *Mirrors surround me.*
> *Cloak me, conceal me.*

Protect me from those
Who wish to betray me.

Flip the picture back over, and hold your hands over it. Charge it with your energy as you imagine a bright, blue protective light glowing all around you. Feel the warmth of this light on your skin while you chant the previous verse nine times. Fold the photo three times, and place it inside the box.

Hold your hands over the slip of paper that has your workplace written on it. Send your energy into the paper as you say nine times:

Nine times over,
Protect what's mine.
Protect what's mine
By the power of nine.
My position at work
Is on lockdown.
I stand strong and proud.
I stand my ground.
My boss can't bring
Him/herself to fire me.
I mean far too much
To this company.

Fold the slip of paper three times, and drop it in the box. Visualize the person who's causing you trouble as you sprinkle in your chosen herb and say:

Sacred herb,
Seal my spell in place.
Get (person's name)
Off my case!

Seal the box closed, saying as you tape each side:

I seal this spell in place.
Get (person's name)
Off my case!

Take the photo of the person who's bothering you at work, and write on the back:

(person's name),
Beneath me,
Below me,
Out of my way.
Stay off my turf.
Stay out of my way.
Banished, bound,
And driven away.
Stay off my turf.
Stay out of my way.

Flip the picture over, and charge it with your energy as you repeat the verse nine times.

Set the mirror box on top of the picture, and leave it there until things have gotten better at work. When you feel like the spell needs a boost, shake the box gently, and repeat nine times:

(person's name),
Beneath me,
Below me,
Out of my way.
Stay off my turf.
Stay out of my way.
Banished, bound,
And driven away.
Stay off my turf.
Stay out of my way.

To Protect Your Relationship

The spell to protect your relationship can be done in two ways. Its first and primary goal is to strengthen the bond that you share with your partner, and then to protect that bond from being sabotaged by inside or outside forces that would drive the two of you apart. This would be a more general application if, say, you didn't know for sure that someone was trying to move in on your partner, or simply wanted to keep the relationship from going wrong. If you do, however, know that someone else is trying to interfere with your relationship — either by trying to break it up, trying to seduce your partner, or trying to cause confusion between the two of you — then you can also use the spell to turn that person's influence back on them, and banish them from your lives.

Care should be taken not to overstep your bounds with this spell. When working with love spells, it can be easy to forget that what you want isn't always what your partner or target has in mind. Never use this spell to impose on someone else's will, or to try to win someone back who you've already lost.

Supplies: A red or pink candle, an outward-facing mirror box, invisible tape, a photo of you and your partner smiling together, a photo of the "other" person (if there is one), a black pen, a small piece of rose quartz, seven rose petals, seven pinches of cinnamon, seven pinches of white sugar, seven small pebbles that you and your partner have picked out specifically for this spell.

By the light of the candle, hold your hands over the photo of you and your partner. Begin charging it with your energy, imagining it glowing with a soft, pink light. As the light grows stronger and brighter in your mind, chant seven times:

As sure as day follows night,
As sure as night follows day,
No one can break us,
Or lead us astray.
Our love stands strong.

Inside the Mirror Box

Our love stands true.
Nothing can part us.
No one can break through.

Place the photo, unfolded, in the box.

Sprinkle in a pinch of sugar, and say:

Sweeter than nectar.

Sprinkle in a pinch of cinnamon, and say:

Hotter than flame.

Drop in a pebble, and say:

Solid as stone.

Let a rose petal drift down into the box, and say:

Yet gentle as rain.

Repeat this process with the herbs and stones a total of seven times.

Hold the rose quartz in your hands, and begin charging it with your energy while you repeat seven times:

Unbendable.
Unbreakable.
Like the stone in my hand.
All darkness and obstacles
Our love will withstand.

Place the stone in the box. Hold your hands over it, and let your energy flow down over the items inside. Imagine the box glowing with the same warm, pink light as before. Repeat seven times:

Sweeter than nectar.
Hotter than flame.
Solid as stone.
Yet gentle as rain.
Our love stands strong.
Our love stands true.
Nothing can part us.
No one can break through.

Continue chanting as you seal the lid on the box with the tape, repeating the chant one more time on each side.

At this point, if you know for a fact that someone is trying to interfere with your relationship, place their photo on the altar (or use a slip of paper with their name written on it). Pick up the black pen, and let the energy in your hand travel down through it. Feel that energy pouring into the paper as you begin drawing a banishing pentagram over the person's face. Trace it again and again while you say nine times:

(person's name),
Beneath me,
Below me,
Out of my way.
Stay off my turf.
Stay out of my way.
Banished, bound,
And driven away.
Stay off my turf.
Stay out of my way.

When you're finished, place the mirror box directly over the unfolded photograph. Wherever you decide to store the box, keep it on top of the photo. When it steals your attention, gently shake it while you repeat seven times:

Inside the Mirror Box

Sweeter than nectar.
Hotter than flame.
Solid as stone.
Yet gentle as rain.
Our love stands strong.
Our love stands true.
Nothing can part us.
No one can break through.

To Make Yourself a Better Person

In the same manner that an inverted mirror box can help someone shine with more confidence and charisma, the outward-facing mirror box can protect a person from displaying more negative traits that might be off-putting to those around them. The difference is in the way the mirrors function in each type of spell. Where the inverted mirror box helps reflect positive energies back on you, the outward-facing mirrors can work in two ways. One idea is that they will deflect and banish negative traits that you want to permanently remove from your personality. The other is that these qualities are symbolically bound so that they no longer have power over you, and then left in the darkness of the box where they're isolated from you. The mirrors will then work to keep you away from those traits to prevent you from picking them up again.

As an introvert, I wrote this spell for people who are painfully shy, or those with high levels of social anxiety. However, it can also be used to banish other traits that create awkward social situations, and might give others a bad impression. Jumping to conclusions, getting angry over trivial things, putting your foot in your mouth, and gossiping are just a few examples of tendencies that the outward facing mirrors can remove from your personality. Getting rid of some of these undesirable behaviors will let others see you for the good person that you are, and give you a more welcoming aura that will attract better people and energy into your life.

A few days before you do the next spell, sit down and write out a list of some of the self-sabotaging qualities that you want to banish from your personality. As always, take your time, and be completely honest with yourself. Accepting your flaws is the best way to understand them, and the first step towards taking action to improve upon them. If you identify with some of the things I've already mentioned, be sure to put those on your list. Write down anything that you want to improve upon, no matter how big or small it might seem. When you're satisfied with the list, transfer it over to a smaller slip of paper that will fit easily inside the mirror box after being folded. Keep the list on your altar until you're ready to cast the spell.

Supplies: A yellow or white candle, an outward-facing mirror box, invisible tape, the list you've prepared of qualities you wish to banish, High John the Conqueror root, red brick dust, a spool of black thread, scissors.

By the light of the candle, hold your hands over the list on your altar. Feel your energy pulsing out of your hands, and flowing into the paper. Say three times:

These are the vices
That I wish to banish.
They only hold me back,
So now I make them vanish!

Read each quality off of your list, one at a time, as part of the next verse:

(quality),
You no longer control me!
Out of my life.
Away with thee!

Fold the paper into a small package, so tiny that it can't be folded anymore. As you fold the paper, say at least nine times:

I seal you up tight.
I lock you away.
You are out of my life.
I banish you away!

156

Once the paper is folded up as small as it can get, begin wrapping it tightly with the black thread while you chant at least nine times:

I bind myself forever
From exhibiting the traits
Scrawled on this page.
I push them down.
I hold them down.
I banish them away!

Wrap the paper in every direction until it's completely covered in multiple layers of thread. Pick up the scissors when you feel ready, and hold them up to the string. Say:

I sever the ties
That bind me
To these negative
And harmful qualities.

Snip the thread from the spool. Drop the package into the box. Sprinkle in three pinches of High John the Conqueror root, saying each time:

Sacred herb,
Breathe life into this working.
Help me overpower
The vices I've been harboring.

Sprinkle in three pinches of red brick dust, saying each time:

Pulverized. Scattered.
Like dust in the wind.
Your reign over my life
Has finally met its end.

Seal the box closed with the tape. Say as you tape down each side:

I seal my vices away from me.
Into the darkness,
Where they cannot affect me.

Keep the box on your altar, or in another inconspicuous place. Each time you feel the need, gently shake the box, and repeat three times:

Keep my vices sealed away from me
In the darkness of this box,
Where they cannot affect me.

To Stop Unwanted Advances

One of the more frequent requests I've received for banishing spells has involved stopping the advances of someone who's coming on too strongly. In most cases, this was someone who had a crush on a friend of mine, and couldn't seem to understand that their feelings were not — and would not ever be — returned. I've also written spells for people whose exes wouldn't stop trying to win them back, and in one case had to banish an ex from a friend's life who was getting violently jealous.

When using the mirror box for this type of spell, the goal is to bind the offender's behavior so that it will stop altogether. The target is then placed inside the outward-facing mirror box where they will be isolated from the person they're harassing. The outward facing mirrors will symbolically deflect the victim away from the target of the spell, while keeping the target bound and gagged inside. The target and the victim become equally repelled from one another so that all ties are severed between them.

The same spell can be turned around on the practitioner to help them control their own impulses when they realize they may be coming on to someone else too strongly. If you notice that you're going a little too far with your advances, and want to cool things down before you wreck a good friendship, you can rewrite the chants so that they're directed at yourself.

Inside the Mirror Box

Supplies: A red or black candle, an outward-facing mirror box, invisible tape, a photo of the target (or their name written on a slip of paper), a black pen, calamus or High John the Conqueror root, a chunk of tiger's eye, black ribbon or thread, scissors.

By the light of the candle, write the following chant on the back of the photo with the black pen:

(person's name),
Don't text me.
Don't call me.
Don't buzz my phone.
Don't come to my job.
Don't come to my home.
I want nothing from you.
Just leave me alone!

Hold your hands over the photo, and repeat the verse nine times while you charge the picture with your energy.

When you're ready, fold the photo three times. Begin wrapping it tightly with the black ribbon or thread. Wrap the photo in every direction until it's completely covered all the way around. As you work, slowly chant nine times:

(person's name),
I bind you from contacting me.
I bind you from making
Advances toward me.
I bind you from harassing me.
I bind your feelings for me.
I banish you away from me.

Once you're finished, pick up the scissors, and hold them against the thread. Say:

Ray Baker

I cut the thread
That connects you to me.
Get me out of your head,
And leave me be.

Snip the thread from the spool. Drop the packet in the mirror box. Sprinkle in the calamus or High John the Conqueror root, and add in the tiger's eye while you repeat nine times:

(person's name),
Get me out of your head,
And leave me be.

Hold your hands over the box. Pour your energy into it while you envision the person isolated in the darkness, unable to escape or bother you. Say nine times:

You're in this box,
All on your own.
Far away from me.
Leaving me alone.

Seal the box closed with the tape, repeating the last verse as you tape down each side. Drip the wax from the burning candle over the lid in the shape of a banishing pentagram.

If you can, keep the box in the freezer to freeze that person's influence out of your life. If this isn't an option, keep the box on the altar, or in another safe place, where you can shake it when it steals your attention. When you shake the box, repeat in sets of three:

(person's name),
Get me out of your head,
And leave me be.

Inside the Mirror Box

For Passive Separation, or Removing Yourself From an Argument

The last spell covered banishing unwanted attention from people who are working too hard to win you over. In this case, the person you're banishing is usually someone you're not already close to (although it could easily be an obsessive ex or overzealous friend). However, there are times when an existing relationship or friendship turns sour, and it's time to cut the remaining ties between you and a former lover or friend. Removing someone from your life that you once cared about is never an easy task. But there are times when it's in the best interest of all parties involved (especially when trying to force yourselves to get along is only creating more animosity).

Version one of the following spell will help you peacefully sever ties with someone who's no longer a good match for you. It uses two outward-facing mirror boxes (one with your name in it, and the other containing the name of your target) to deflect you away from each other, and gradually push you apart. It focuses strongly on passive separation so that no harm will come to either party, and no negativity will grow between you. You'll simply drift apart so that you can go your separate ways.

Before doing the first version of this spell, be sure that you're ready to remove the other person from your life. The working is meant to put up permanent walls between you. Once the other person is gone, you might not ever get a chance to see or speak to them again. If your goal centers more around an extended break from one another, then this spell isn't a good option. Try placing their name under a plate instead, and then burn a light blue candle over it to help cool things down for a while.

Version two of the spell focuses on separating you from an argument in which you never should've been involved. Like the spell for passive separation, the second version uses two mirror boxes. The outward-facing mirror box is meant to protect the practitioner from the people who are arguing, and to deflect any negative effects that the fight might have on them. The inverted mirror box should be used on the people who are fighting, so that they will be left alone with their own troubles until they can come to a peaceful resolution. The two boxes are then gradually moved apart to temporarily separate the practitioner from the targets until things settle back down.

Be advised that things might get a little rough for those who are participating in the fight. Stand your ground, and don't let yourself get drawn back into it. You can always take the inverted mirror box apart for a while if things get too rough. However, you should keep yourself in the outward-facing box to avoid being sucked back into the fight. Only take both boxes apart when you're confident that the situation has been completely resolved.

Version One: Passive Separation

Supplies: A white candle, two outward-facing mirror boxes, invisible tape, a photo of each person that will be separated (if you have a photo of both of you together, bring scissors to the altar so that you can cut the picture in half during the spell), black pepper or dragon's blood herb.

Light the candle in the name of peace. If you have one photo of you and the person you wish to separate from, cut the two of you apart as you say three times (if using a separate picture of each of you, simply move them a few inches apart while you chant):

> *I am now separated*
> *From (person's name).*
> *I seal tight this spell.*
> *Between (person's name) and I,*
> *Bring a peaceful farewell.*

Hold your hands over your own photo. Pour your energy into it, and see yourself walking away from the other person. Say nine times:

> *(person's name),*
> *I banish myself from your influence.*
> *I banish myself from your sphere.*
> *Peacefully, I walk away from us.*
> *The bond between us disappears.*

162

Add your picture to the first mirror box. Sprinkle in three pinches of black pepper or dragon's blood as you say three times:

Sacred herb,
Seal tight this spell.
Between (person's name) and I,
Bring a peaceful farewell.

Tape the first box shut, saying on each side:

I am forever isolated
From (person's name).
I seal tight this spell.
Between (person's name) and I,
Bring a peaceful farewell.

Place the first box in the center of the altar. Hold your hands over the picture of the other person. Pour your energy into it, and see that person walking away from you without looking back. As they get smaller and smaller in the distance, say nine times:

(person's name),
I banish you from my influence.
I banish you from my sphere.
Peacefully, you walk away from us.
The bond between us disappears.

Drop the photo into the second mirror box. Sprinkle in three pinches of black pepper or dragon's blood as you say three times:

Sacred herb,
Seal tight this spell.
Between (person's name) and I,
Bring a peaceful farewell.

Tape the second box shut, saying on each side:

(person's name),
Is now isolated from me.
I seal tight this spell.
Between (person's name) and I,
Bring a peaceful farewell.

Place the second box on the altar, and arrange both of them so that they're up against one another. Hold your hands over both boxes. As you charge them with your energy, say three times:

Every day, and in every way,
We grow farther and farther apart.
Peacefully and quietly,
I break the bond between our hearts.

Move the boxes an inch apart, and leave them there. Each day, repeat the last chant three times, and move the boxes another inch apart. Repeat this process until the boxes are on opposite sides of the altar. Leave them there until you're sure the tie has been permanently severed (one month should be sufficient). If any unwanted activity resumes after you take the boxes apart, repeat the spell immediately.

Version Two: Removing Yourself from an Argument

Supplies: A white candle, an outward-facing mirror box, an inverted mirror box, a photo of each person who's arguing, a photo of yourself (or separate slips of paper with each name written on them), black pepper, rosemary leaves.

Light the candle in the name of peace. Hold your hands over the photo of yourself. As you charge it with your energy, visualize yourself surrounded by a bright, electric blue protective light. See the light get stronger and stronger as you say nine times:

I am protected from words
And actions that are not my doing.

Inside the Mirror Box

Protected from hurt feelings and slurs
In this fight that's brewing.
I will have no part
In quarrels that are not my own.
(person's name) and (other person's name),
I want no part in your fight.
Now, leave me alone!

Place your photo inside the outward-facing mirror box. Sprinkle in nine rosemary leaves, and say three times:

Sacred herb,
Seal tight my spell.
Get me out of the middle
Of this senseless quarrel.

Seal the box closed with the tape, repeating the last verse on each side. Place the box in the center of the altar.

I seal the box.
I seal tight my spell.
Get me out of the middle
Of this senseless quarrel.

Now place your hands over the photos of the people who are fighting. As you send your energy into the photos, imagine those people slowly lifting off of the ground, and moving away from you. As they move farther away in your mind, imagine their bickering voices fading off into the distance. Make your visualization stronger as you say nine times:

Get out of my life.
Get out of my way.
Until you've both
Learned to behave.
I will not be pulled in.
I will not take sides.

I will not take part
In your little fight.
May you both be guided
To a peaceful resolution.
But keep me off your minds
Until you've found the solution.

Place both pictures inside the inverted mirror box. Sprinkle in three pinches of black pepper, and say three times:

Sacred herb,
Seal tight my spell.
Get me out of the middle
Of this senseless quarrel.

Begin sealing the box closed with the tape. Say as you seal each side:

I am removed from the fight
In which you've indulged.
Until you've worked things out,
You will leave me alone!

Place the second box on the altar, up against the first one. Move the boxes one inch apart, and repeat the last verse three more times. Repeat this process every day until the fight has ended, and it's safe to resume talking to the people involved.

To Define Personal Boundaries

The spell to define personal boundaries can be used when banishing a particular person might not be an option. When dealing with bosses, classmates, and relatives, for example, it isn't always as easy as banishing someone from your life and walking away. There are also times when you want to cool down a person's behavior toward you, but banishing them or hitting them with a return to sender spell is too harsh of a reaction. Maybe you really do want to maintain a friendship or

166

relationship with someone, but they need to learn to respect certain personal boundaries that you have in place. Flirtatious coworkers, a partner who's moving too fast, or a friend who tends to take way more than they give would all be good targets for this spell. Think of it as a magickal way of saying, "I love you to death, but you need to chill."

Before casting, sit down with a pen and paper. Concentrate on your target, and think about the frustrating ways in which they step out of bounds with you. Translate these frustrations into short phrases on your list that can easily be written on your mirrors. Keep the list in a safe place until the time comes to cast the spell. Remember not to construct the box or write on the mirrors yet, as you'll be performing these actions as part of the working.

After casting, be prepared for a certain degree of confrontation. If you haven't been able to talk to that person about how they've been acting, this spell might open the door to a respectful conversation about your limitations and personal boundaries. This could happen when the words you've been searching for finally come to you, or through that person's own realization that they've been stepping out of bounds. However it plays out, try to keep things as respectful and peaceful as possible without sacrificing your own needs.

Supplies: A black candle, an outward-facing mirror box, invisible tape, a favorite photo of yourself, a photo of your target, a list of ways that your target has been overstepping your personal boundaries, nine cloves, a fine-tipped black permanent marker, a spool of black string, a pair of scissors.

By the light of the black candle, spread the mirrors out on the altar (reflective side up). Using the permanent marker, write the name of your target at the top of each mirror. Call out their name three times each time you write it, and see that person clearly in your mind.

Next, transfer the items from your list onto the mirrors. If you have less than six things listed, you can write the most frustrating ones more than once. If you have more than six (and you're still not seriously considering a banishing spell), write more than one item on each mirror. Continue to concentrate on that person as you work, and on the different ways that they disrespect your boundaries.

When you're finished, hold your hands over the mirrors on your altar. Let the energy from your palms flow down over the mirrors as you say nine times:

(person's name),
These are the ways
In which you overstep
My personal boundaries.
From this point forward,
These lines will not be crossed.
You WILL respect me.

Begin constructing the mirror box as you would for any other working. Leave the lid off until the end of the spell, and be careful not to smudge or remove any of your writing with your fingers. While you work, chant in sets of three:

(person's name),
You WILL respect me.

Set the box aside when it's ready. Place the photo of yourself in front of you. Hold your hands over the picture, and let the energy from your palms flow down into it. While you work, imagine yourself glowing with a bright, protective light. Say nine times:

I demand respect
For myself and all that's mine.
The mirrors rise up around me.
My boundaries they define.

Fold your photo three times, and add it to the box.

Hold the cloves in the palm of your hand, and charge them while you say three times:

Sacred herb,
Breathe life into my spell.
Activate my protective force field.

Sprinkle the cloves into the box. Hold your hands over it, and let your energy charge it with a bright, protective light. Chant nine times:

Mirrors,
Rise up.
Mirrors,
Surround me.
Define the lines
Of my personal boundaries.
No one can cross
The lines I've defined.
I demand respect
For me and mine.
Should anyone dare
To cross these bounds,
Block them.
Deflect them.
Shut them down.

When you're ready, seal the lid on the box while repeating on each side:

Should anyone dare
To cross these bounds,
Block them.
Deflect them.
Shut them down.

Take your spool of black string, and loop it around the mirror box. Tie it off with a knot, and then begin slowly wrapping the string around the box in different directions. There doesn't need to be a set pattern or design, and you can weave the string in and out of itself if you choose. The point is to create a tangled web of string on the outside of the box that will represent the personal lines you've laid down during the spell. While you work, chant nine times:

As this black string
Is wrapped and wound,
It defines the lines
Of my personal bounds.
I wrap this black string
Around and around.
My personal boundaries
I firmly set down.
No one can cross
This web that I've wound.
Lest they be banished.
Lest they be bound.

Tie off the string, and cut it from the spool with the scissors. Set the box aside for now.

Place the photo of your target in front of you. Slowly trace a banishing pentagram nine times over their photo with the tip of your finger. As you do so, imagine the energy in your hand flowing down through your finger, and into the picture. Repeat nine times:

(person's name),
Don't overstep my bounds.
Don't even dare to cross me.
You WILL respect my space,
And you WILL respect me.

Without folding it, firmly place the mirror box over the person's photo. Say:

Inside the Mirror Box

It is done!

Leave the box there. When you feel like you need to recharge the spell, shake it gently while repeating the last chant, and always firmly place the box back down on the photo.

To Block Hatred

I originally wrote this working to protect myself from all forms of hatred and negativity. As someone who has spent many years working with the general public, I know exactly how nasty some people can be when they think they have authority over another person. Whether you work as a server, bartender, cashier, in retail, or any other customer-based position, you'll inevitably encounter "that" customer. The person who will use the "paying customer" card as an opportunity to fully abuse the little bit of power that they have over you for the short time you have the pleasure of knowing them.

Sadly, this isn't the only time you might encounter this kind of negativity. The hatred you're dealing with might be coming from your own boss, coworkers, classmates, or even relatives. If you have a specific person (or group of people) in mind for this spell, you can always work names into the chants, and include photographs or personal effects when you perform it. Additionally, if you've noticed that you've been getting carried away with your own negative emotions, you can rewrite the verses to bind yourself from being hateful toward other people.

Supplies: A white candle, an outward-facing mirror box, invisible tape, a small vial that will fit inside the mirror box, a small slip of paper that can be rolled up inside the vial, a black pen, brown sugar, honey.

Light the candle in the name of love and protection. Write your name on the slip of paper, making the letters thick and dark as you trace over them.

Hold your hands over the paper, and see it glowing in your mind with bright, protective light. As you charge it, say eleven times:

Ray Baker

I'm surrounded by love.
As this light starts to grow,
Hatred falls dead
In this spell's loving glow.

Roll the paper into a small tube, and slide it into the vial. Carefully fill it halfway with honey, and then the rest of the way with brown sugar.

Cap the vial, and begin to roll it back and forth between your palms. Send your energy into it, and let it begin to glow with loving, protective light in your mind's eye. As you do so, say eleven times:

Protection and love,
Stick fast to me.
Keep my life sweet
Like sugar and honey.
Sticky and sweet,
Keep evil at bay.
Trap all hatred,
And turn it away.

Place the vial in the mirror box. Hold your hands over it, and let your energy pour down from your palms while you say eleven times:

Mirrors,
Surround me.
Turn the tides.
Block others' hatred
On all sides.

Seal the box closed with the tape. Repeat as you seal each side:

Should any hatred
Try to come my way,
Deflect it. Block it.
Send it away.

Keep the box in a safe place, and shake it when you need extra protection from negative people and their influence.

To Break Bad Habits and Addictions

Most people have some sort of bad habit or addiction that has become part of their daily routine, and in some cases, comes to define who they are. Some bad habits are harmless, and are simply annoying both to yourself and those around you. Smacking gum, chewing with your mouth wide open, or biting your nails all fall into this category. Other habits, such as drinking, smoking, or drug use, can get out of hand quickly, and consume a person's life to the point that they put their health and well-being at risk.

No matter what you're struggling with, the next spell is written to help break the mental hold that your bad habit or addiction has over you. Similar to the glamour spells in chapter four, this working aims to change the thought patterns that keep you reaching for that bag of cookies, or lighting up that next cigarette. It also attempts to isolate you from the habit so that it will be easier to give it up. It affirms in your mind that your bad habit is powerless against you.

One of the primary supplies for this spell will be something small that symbolizes your bad habit or addiction. Most habits leave behind some kind of paraphernalia that will make a great token to throw in the box. For smoking, use a cigarette butt. Save a wine cork or the tab off of a beer can for drinking. For gambling or over-spending, use an old lottery ticket or shopping receipt. Let your creativity guide you when searching for a small representation that will fit inside the box.

As I was typing up the next spell, I realized that the same working can be used to escape from an abusive relationship. The verses can be used as is. Just call out the target's name where you would otherwise name the addiction. In place of the token representing a bad habit, use a photo of the person from whom you need to escape. The spell will put a barrier between you and the other person, and help you mentally and physically escape from their influence.

Supplies: A white candle, an outward-facing mirror box, invisible tape, a token that symbolizes your bad habit or addiction, red brick dust, graveyard dirt, a broken necklace chain.

By the light of the white candle, hold the token in your dominant hand, and charge it with your energy. Feel the object grow hot in your hand. Say nine times:

> *For all this time,*
> *You've had your hold on me.*
> *But I have the power*
> *To set myself free.*
> *I raise up within me*
> *The strength to break free.*
> *You have no power over me.*

Continue charging the object, exerting all of your power over it, as you repeat nine more times:

> *You have no power over me.*

Drop the token in the box. Pick up the necklace chain, and begin violently tearing it into small pieces. As you tear the chain and throw the pieces in the box, call out at least nine times:

> *(addiction/habit),*
> *I break the chains*
> *That bind me to you.*
> *I sever the ties.*
> *I unstick the glue.*

When you're ready, sprinkle in nine pinches of red brick dust. Say each time:

> *(addiction/habit),*
> *I set myself free.*

Inside the Mirror Box

You are nothing more
Than dust at my feet.

Sprinkle in nine pinches of graveyard dirt, saying each time:

(addiction/habit),
I seal you in your grave.
Your hold over me
Has passed away.

Hold your hands over the box. Send your energy into it, and say nine times:

(addiction/habit),
You have no power over me.
I have finally been set free.

Seal the box closed with the tape, repeating the last verse on each side. Keep the box somewhere safe where you can access it easily. Any time you feel the urge to indulge in your bad habit or addiction, shake the box gently for five minutes, and repeat the last verse as many times as you like. If you can't access the box, sneak off to the restroom or another place where you can spend a few moments alone. Close your eyes, and quietly repeat the chant until the urge has passed. Repeat as necessary until the habit has been broken.

The Star Shield Meditation

The star shield meditation isn't a physical mirror box spell, but rather a meditation that can be performed in the practitioner's mind in any place and at any time that extra protection is needed. I recommend recording it (or having a friend record it for you if you get uncomfortable listening to your own voice), and using the recording the first few times you perform it. The meditation should be done in the comfort of the home until you're able to remember the general flow of the imagery, and are able to easily call it up without using the recording. Once memorized, it can easily be shortened to its basic images, and performed on the fly while parked in the car, at work, out in public, or in any other situation that extra protection is needed.

For the full meditation, close the curtains and turn off the lights, or sit in a dark room by the light of a single candle. Begin by sitting or lying in a comfortable position with your arms and legs uncrossed. If a friend is reading or recording the meditation, have them read only the section in quotation marks. Be sure they read slowly and quietly, and that the room is free of outside noises and distractions both when the meditation is recorded, and any time you perform it at home. It may not always be possible to perform it in public without distractions, but at that point you should be able to visualize it fairly quickly and discretely, without anyone even noticing that you're not fully in the present moment.

"Let your eyes drift upward, and find a spot on the ceiling on which you can casually concentrate. Take three deep, relaxing breaths. Let your lungs fill completely with air as you inhale, and then let them empty completely as you exhale. On the third breath, let your eyelids slowly close.

Continue breathing in the same fashion as you begin to let your entire body relax. Concentrate first on your feet. As you breathe in and out, let the muscles in your toes and feet relax completely. With each breath you take, let the sensation of relaxation move farther up into your calves, then past your knees, and now into your thighs. Breathe in again. As you exhale, let the tension in your torso fall away. Let the relaxation travel up through your abdominal muscles, and into your chest. Continue breathing. Feel the tenseness in your shoulders let go. Let that sensation travel down into your arms, feeling them become limp and relaxed all the way to the tips of your fingers. Take another deep breath. As you let it out, allow the tension in your neck to go with it. Let your head go limp as your neck relaxes, and know that all of the tension and stress has left your body. Continue breathing for a moment, and just enjoy the feeling of complete and total relaxation.

In your mind's eye, you see that you're standing at the top of a large staircase. A red carpet travels down the center of this staircase, and opens up into a dark room ten steps below. You decide you want to see what's in that room, so you take a deep breath, and step down onto the tenth step. You realize that you feel even more relaxed than you did before, and that you've gone a little bit farther down into your subconscious mind. You take another deep breath, and step down onto the ninth step. You feel even more relaxed than when you were on step ten, and feel even more submerged in your subconscious mind. Taking your time, and enjoying the feeling of complete relaxation, you take a deep breath again, and step down onto the eighth step. You breathe in again, and step down onto the seventh step, feeling more and more relaxed with each step you take. Breathe in, and step down onto the sixth step, sinking farther and farther into your subconscious mind. Step down, now, onto the fifth step, falling deeper and deeper into relaxation. After another deep, relaxing breath, you step down onto the fourth step. You're feeling so relaxed now that nothing can bother you. The worries of the day have disappeared, and you know that once you get to that room at the end of the stairs, that room that lies in the depths of your subconscious mind, you'll be able to achieve anything you desire. You step down again onto the third step. You feel your subconscious opening up before you as you get closer and closer to the end of the staircase. You take another deep breath, and step down onto the second step. Deeper into relaxation, and even deeper into your subconscious mind. You step down onto the first step. You're at your deepest level of relaxation now. You see that the red carpet continues into the dimly lit room before you, inviting you to follow it inside. After another nice, deep breath, you step down onto the carpet, and walk toward the open doorway that leads to your subconscious mind.

Upon entering this room, you see that it's very dark. Only a vague, pulsating light shines through a thick haze that surrounds you as you walk in. You search for the source of this light, and you quickly notice that it's coming from a spot on the floor at the center of the room. You approach this light. The closer you get, the brighter the light becomes, and the thinner the haze that surrounds you. After a few steps, the haze has completely disappeared, and you realize that the bright light is coming from a large five-point star embedded in the floor of the room. Its bright column of light shines up into the darkness. It's warm and pulsing, and is inviting you to come closer. You step onto the center of the star. The bright, protective light shines all around you. You feel its warmth on your skin. You feel it attaching to you, and soaking into you. You sit down in the center of the star, soaking up its glow with every deep breath you take.

Suddenly, you see another bright light on the floor in front of you, just to the left of where you're sitting. This light moves all the way to the right, creating a bright line in front of you at the top of the star. The line makes a sharp turn that traces another line along the right of the glowing star. The line turns again, and continues across the bottom two points, and then again to complete a square all the way around the star. As the square glows brightly in the darkness, a new line comes up from each corner, and makes its way straight up into the air above you. The lines stop just above your head, where they each branch out to connect with one another. You now see that a cube made of bright, pulsating lines surrounds you.

On each wall of the cube, you see that five-point stars are beginning to materialize out of thin air. They're all different sizes, but made of the same light as the star beneath you, and as the box that now surrounds you. As the stars glow brighter and brighter, their light begins to connect them to one another so that the darkness outside the box is no longer visible. Although the light is bright, it doesn't hurt your eyes. And although its warmth is strong, you feel that it's comfortable and inviting. You let the light grow brighter and brighter. You know that nothing can penetrate these walls of pure, protective energy that now surround you. You know that no evil can get to you. No negativity can affect you. So long as you're surrounded in this pure shield of starlight, you remain impenetrable on all planes of existence. You're impervious to danger of all kinds in mind, body, and spirit. Nothing can get to you. No one can harm you.

You bask in this light for a moment longer, letting it soak into you from every direction. Feeling its warmth course through your body along your chakra centers. Knowing that it's coursing through your veins. Now that the light has completely engulfed you, you see that it slowly starts to diminish. It grows dimmer and dimmer, and although this protective box of light is fading fast in your mind's eye, you know that it's still there. You know it's still working hard to protect you, even when you can't see it with your eyes. The light continues to fade. The darkness of the room becomes visible again as the stars disappear one by one. Slowly vanishing from your sight, but leaving their warmth and protection behind. The box is nearly gone now, leaving only the glowing star beneath you on the floor.

But even this star begins to fade away, and as it does, you become aware, again, of your body. Of your fingers and your toes. Your legs. Your arms. Your neck and your head. The sounds of the room begin to fade back in. You hear the sound of my voice beckoning you out of the darkness. You follow it back up. Slowly back up. Back up into the present moment. You know that when you hear me count to three, you'll have no choice but to open your eyes, and awake. One … two … three. Awake."

Star Shield Meditation: Short Version

This version is intended for use in public once you get the hang of the full meditation. It's more discrete, and performed much more quickly. It can be used in situations where you see danger coming, but still have time to work to protect yourself. I usually do it when I see that things are about to get heated between people out in public, or when I'm dealing with a customer who is about to get out of hand. I've also done it when I knew that I was about to walk into a touchy situation that I wasn't able to avoid, and before difficult conversations with friends. While doing the meditation in my mind, I also take steps on a physical level to either diffuse the negative energies that are building, or remove myself from the situation altogether.

If you can, excuse yourself to the restroom, your car, or step outside for a moment. If the situation you're in doesn't allow this, simply find an object or spot on the wall to concentrate on, and stare at it for a quick moment. As you do, take three deep, relaxing breaths, and let your eyes close briefly on the third breath (I pretend that I'm yawning so that bystanders don't think anything about what I'm doing). Feel your consciousness instantly drop into a daydreamy state. Open your eyes now if you need to, but continue the visualization in your mind.

Skip the stairway visualization, and imagine that when your mind's eye opens, you're standing in the dim room deep in your subconscious mind. You instantly notice that you're standing over your protective five-point star, and that it's warm light is already glowing all around you. The square of light quickly traces its way around the star on the floor, and then extends up and over you on all sides to form the bright cube of pulsating light. Without missing a beat, the glowing stars begin to appear on the walls of the cube. Their light grows stronger and brighter. You feel the warmth on your skin as the light becomes so bright that the stars are no longer visible. Bask in this protective light for a short moment, and let it form an impenetrable shield around you.

When you're ready, let this light fade away in your mind. Return to your normal state, but know that the protective energy of the star shield is still all around you. Know that it's still working hard to keep you safe in whatever situation you've found yourself.

When a Spell Has Run Its Course:
Ending Mirror Box Spells

Every spell has a shelf life. Like any type of magick, spells done with the mirror box will eventually run their course, and will need to be brought to an official close by the practitioner. The primary reason for closing any spell is to stop the flow of energy being fed into it, and to allow that energy to be released back to what I call the Universal Power Grid, or the constantly recycled system of potential and kinetic energies that exists throughout the universe. Additionally, by ritually closing the spell, the practitioner affirms the end of the working in their mind. They let go of their attachment to it, thereby breaking their mental hold over the target. This is considered by some witches to be the most important part of the process, since the mind is what creates and drives the spell in the first place.

There are as many ways to close a spell as there are ways to cast one. The methods used will vary from practitioner to practitioner, but oftentimes depend on how the spell worked (or didn't work) in a particular situation. Most spells naturally come to an end simply because the energies that were cast out have done their assigned task. Once the job is done, the energy that once gave it life has no reason to stick around. Most of the energies will return to their place in the cycle to be used again for other purposes. Still, there can always be residual energies running in the background that could continue to affect the practitioner or target if they're not released. No matter how the spell played out, it's always a good idea to perform a small ritual to lay the working to rest.

Some spells — like many of those in chapters four and five — are actually designed to keep working over an extended period of time, but become stagnant when energy isn't being fed into them on a regular basis. The spells in this book are "recharged" by gently tapping or shaking the box while reciting the verse from the original working. Doing so feeds the spells new energy, and reinforces the original intent. This doesn't just work with the mirror box, either. The life of any spell can be extended in a similar fashion until the practitioner decides that it's time to formally close it.

Then there are spells that fail. There are many reasons that a spell can be considered a failure. It might have lacked the energy needed to get off the ground, or it might have yielded undesirable results. The spell might have even backfired, or in the case of the spells in this book, the mirror box might have ended up breaking. Spells that don't work out should be brought to a close as soon as possible to clear the air, and set the stage for a fresh start should the practitioner want to give it another shot. Even if you're dismantling the box to give everyone involved a breather, you should still perform a closing ritual to officially end the previous round.

Demagicking the Box

The first step in closing a mirror box spell is to demagick the box and the remains of the spell so that they can then be either cleansed and reused, or completely disposed of. With other types of spells, demagicking can be as simple as burning a slip of paper, burying the ends of candles at the base of a tree, or emptying the contents of a mojo bag into a living body of water. Mirror boxes, however, leave behind a lot of items that aren't always burnable or biodegradable. These materials must be handled accordingly to prevent environmental pollution and possible injury to wildlife.

Begin the demagicking ritual by lighting a stick of your favorite incense. Sit in front of the altar with the mirror box in the center. Take a moment to breathe deeply, and enjoy the scent of the smoke. Let it take you down into a state of deep, but focused, relaxation. When you feel ready, use the index finger of your subordinate hand to trace a banishing pentagram three times over the top of the box. If you wish to draw a circle around the pentagram, do so in a counterclockwise direction. As you slowly trace the symbol, imagine the energies in and around the box detaching from it, and dissipating into the air. As you perform these actions, say three times:

I return the power
That I raised during this spell
Back to its place in the universe.
The energies flow back
Into the sacred well
As they become neutralized,
Detached, and dispersed.

Use a bolline, pocket knife, or the tip of a pair of scissors to carefully cut the seal around the lid of the mirror box. Place the open box back on the altar. Using your hand or a large feather, gently waft the smoke from the incense stick into box. Move in counterclockwise circles as you recite the previous verse three more times.

Now that you've demagicked the box, you can go about cleansing and disposing of the materials that are left behind. I usually dump the contents of the box into my cauldron (I use a large clay bowl that a friend made for me in a pottery class), and take out any coins, stones, or other items that will not burn or naturally break down. Then I completely dismantle the box, and try to remove as much of the tape, wax, et cetera as possible. I bury the mirrors and the other items I placed aside in a bowl full of salt for at least one moon cycle. When the moon cycle is complete, the cleansed items can be removed from the salt bath to be used again for other spells, or for other purposes altogether.

I dispose of any other materials (locks of hair, spell papers, photos, herbs, et cetera) using one or more of the four elements. Each element has its own properties that release stored energy from an object by destroying it. The nature of the materials will oftentimes determine which element (or which combination of elements) is used to destroy the remaining spell scraps. Each has their benefits and pitfalls, but they all essentially perform the same task: releasing the energy that was attached to the items during the spell, and breaking the tie between the personal effects or correspondences and the target.

Earth

Earth destroys via the natural process of decomposition. As biodegradable objects rot in the ground, their stored energy is released into the soil, and converted into nutrients for plants and some forms of animal life. Materials that can't decompose — or do so very slowly — can still be neutralized using the element of Earth. It's believed that soil or salt strips the objects of their energies, and allows those energies to dissipate away (thus the concept behind burying magickal objects in salt or soil in order to cleanse them).

One way to use Earth to dispose of magickal remains is to take a late night stroll near the river, through a park, or in another wooded area. Be sure to bring a digging spade or shovel, as well as a small container of natural sea salt. Under the privacy of the night, find a triangle of healthy trees that are roughly an equal distance apart. It might take a while to find the right trees, but keep your mind open, and let the trees attract you to them. When you've found the right spot, dig a hole at the center of the triangle. Dump the spell remains into the hole, and take a few deep breaths. With the index finger of your subordinate hand, begin tracing a banishing pentagram or spiral three times over the hole, and say three times:

By the element of Earth,
I lay to rest the energies
That once breathed life
Into my magick spell.
I give them back to the universe,
And I bid them farewell.

As you recite the verse, imagine that the items in the hole are glowing faintly. Allow this glow to seep into the soil, where it spreads out in the direction of the three trees until it becomes thin, and finally disappears. Sprinkle in three pinches of sea salt. Cover the hole, and trace a banishing pentagram in the loose soil with the index finger of your subordinate hand. Announce:

It is done.

Now, simply gather your things, and walk away. Know that your work is done.

I prefer a triangle of trees, because the triangle helps me visualize the energies being separated and neutralized as the tree roots pull them up into their trunks. I also like to bury spell remains off of my property whenever possible in order to mentally distance myself from the original working. However, it's perfectly acceptable to bury spell scraps in your favorite potted plant, at the base of a healthy tree, or in a garden or flowerbed where nutrients are being taken up from the soil to sustain life.

A more traditional approach would be to bury items at a crossroads. This works on the same idea as the triangle of trees in that the energy associated with the spell will be scattered in every direction. Unfortunately, in today's world of paved roads and busy neighborhoods, it can be hard to find a suitable crossroads at which to bury your paraphernalia. Even a dirt road can be too hard to dig into, not to mention that prying neighbors might find it suspicious. If you have access to a crossroads in a wooded area or quiet bike trail, you can use that. If not, one of the other options will also work.

Water

Water destroys by dissolving or eroding things away. As the items break apart, their energies are released into the body of water where they were scattered, never to come together in the same place or time again. The key to using the element of Water is to always use a living, moving body. If you live near the ocean, this is absolutely the best option. The vastness of the ocean symbolizes the energies getting lost in the great abyss, never to return. A river or stream is the second best choice, as many rivers eventually lead to the ocean. A lake will also work fine. I do advise against small ponds, puddles, or other stagnant waters. Smaller sources of water tend to be still and dirty, and will probably not exist long enough to completely break down or carry away the items you wish to destroy.

When you have decided on the body of water you wish to use, take your spell remains to that sacred place, and toss them into the water. As you watch them sink or float away, repeat the release chant three times:

By the element of Water,
I wash away the energies
That once breathed life
Into my magick spell.
I give them back to the universe,
And I bid them farewell.

Visualize the water extinguishing and scattering the energies that once clung to the items. Watch them disappear into the moving body. Once they're completely out of sight, say:

It is done.

Walk away, and know that your work is done.

Remember that oceans, rivers, and lakes are delicate ecosystems that all forms of life – including humans – depend on for survival. Only use this method for items that are non-toxic and completely biodegradable. Never throw glass, plastic, rubber, et cetera into a living body of water. Save these things for a salt bath, then reuse or properly dispose of them at a later time.

Fire

Fire destroys by using the stored energy in materials as fuel, thereby consuming and releasing it in the process. A household fireplace, fire pit, or chimenea will all work perfectly for a release ritual. If your cauldron is big enough, you can set it in a safe place outside, and burn your spell scraps in that, although you'll need lighter fluid or another propellant to help them burn.

If you're using a fireplace or fire pit, sit in front of the fire, and take a few deep breaths as you meditate on the flames. When you feel ready, toss the scraps into the fire. As you watch the flames consume them, recite the release chant three times:

> *By the element of Fire,*
> *I burn away the energies*
> *That once breathed life*
> *Into my magick spell.*
> *I give them back to the universe,*
> *And I bid them farewell.*

When the items have been completely consumed, say:

> *It is done.*

Let the rest of the fire burn itself out, and know that your work is done.

If you're using your cauldron, lightly douse the materials with lighter fluid or rubbing alcohol. Ignite them with a cigarette lighter or matches, and recite the release chant as they succumb to the flames. Add more propellant as necessary to help them burn completely. Once the ashes have completely cooled, scatter them to the wind and say:

> *It is done.*

Gather your things. Walk away, and know that your work is done.

Air

Air is the trickiest of the four elements when it comes to disposing of spell scraps. Air typically destroys in the form of strong winds or tornadoes, in which things are torn apart, and then scattered in different directions. Air can also erode things away, but over a much longer period of time than some of the other elements. These aspects of the element are both difficult and dangerous to harness for a demagicking ritual (and would be entirely too strong for these purposes, anyway). However, Air can be used in the form of smudge smoke to release the energies from an object, and by then combining it with fire to turn the remains to ashes that can be given to the wind.

To perform the demagicking ritual using Air, you'll need to bring a smudge stick (or a stick of your favorite incense), a large feather or paper fan, a lighter, lighter fluid or rubbing alcohol, and a cauldron or earthenware bowl containing the items you wish to dispose of. As you would do in the Fire ritual, take these supplies to a safe outdoor area. Light the smudge stick with the lighter. Let it burn for a moment to get it started, then blow out the flame. Use gentle breaths to fuel the embers on the stick so that it smolders, and puts off a thick cloud of smoke.

Moving in counterclockwise circles, gently waft the smoke into the bowl of scraps with the feather or fan. Say three times:

By the element of Air,
I smudge away the energies
That once breathed life
Into my magick spell.
I give them back to the universe,
And I bid them farewell.

Visualize the energies attached to the remains being erased away as the smoke flows over them. When you feel ready, extinguish the smudge stick in the dirt, and save it for another smudging ritual. Lightly douse the items in the bowl with propellant, and ignite them with the lighter. Carefully add more propellant as necessary to help the items burn completely.

Once the ashes have cooled, scatter them to the wind, and say:

It is done.

Gather your things. Walk away, and know that your work is done.

Inside the Mirror Box

If a Mirror Box Breaks

In my opinion, breaking a mirror box – even if it was on accident – is a sign that a particular spell has ended itself. Most likely, the box has broken because the spell has done its job, and you're being told that it's time to stop feeding energy into it. It can also mean that the time is just not right for that particular working, or that you're causing unintentional or unmerited harm to others (possibly even people who weren't involved in the original spell, but have somehow found themselves in the crossfire). You may never know the exact reason why a spell shuts itself down, but you should always know that whatever the reason, it's a good one. If this happens to you with one of your mirror boxes, the flow of energy should be stopped immediately, and then the box destroyed.

Closing a spell when a box breaks is similar to a regular demagicking ritual, with the exception that the entire box and its contents must be ritually destroyed and disposed of. I only use the element of Earth in this situation, as it's the least destructive to the environment, and causes the least amount of pollution. Water isn't a good option, since the broken glass and other materials inside the box could potentially harm wildlife, or even people who decide to take a swim in the river or lake in which you tossed the broken glass. Fire usually won't work, either, as most people don't have the means to get a backyard fire hot enough to completely melt down the glass, metal, and other materials inside the box. The items could be smudged with Air, but would still need to be disposed of in some way after the cleansing ritual. Earth, however, allows the materials to be safely buried in a discrete area that's unlikely to be disturbed by humans or animals.

When using Earth to dispose of a broken mirror box, take the entire box (unopened), a digging spade, thick leather gloves, safety glasses, and a small container of natural sea salt to your chosen wooded area. As you would do in the regular closing ritual, find a triangle of trees that are roughly the same distance apart. Dig a hole at least one foot deep by one foot wide. Wearing protective gloves and safety goggles, drop the box into the hole, and begin breaking it apart with the sharp point of the digging spade. Work in short, firm stabbing motions so that the glass shatters, but pieces don't fly up into your face, or hit your body. Check between each jab to ensure that shards of glass aren't sticking up waiting to gouge the side of your hand. As you carefully break the box apart, say three times slowly:

I shatter this box.
I scatter its power
Back into the Earth,
Where it will be devoured.
Unwound and unbound,
Release the magick within.
Return the power to the sacred grid.

Sprinkle in three pinches of sea salt. Cover the hole, and trace a banishing pentagram in the loose soil with the index finger of your subordinate hand. Announce:

It is done.

Gather your things, and walk away. Know that your work is done.

Breaking a Mirror Box Spell

Aside from spells ending themselves or needing to be closed, there will inevitably come a time when you want to break or reverse a spell that has given undesirable results. Rituals to break or reverse spells are typically only done when a working backfires, inadvertently causes harm to one or more people, or when the practitioner has second thoughts after casting. Closing a spell and breaking a spell are two very distinct things. When closing a working, you're affirming that you wish for the spell to cease action, and to be laid to rest. The flow of energy is cut off without further affecting the outcome of the spell. Breaking a spell, however, entails both stopping the flow of energy, and attempting to reverse the effects that have already, or soon will, take place.

The most difficult part of breaking or reversing a spell is attempting to undo any harm that has already been done. While the first part of breaking a spell entails shutting down the working, the second part works to repair the negative effects that the target, the practitioner, or anyone else involved has had to endure. With any luck, you'll see that the spell is going wrong before too much damage is done, and will be able to stop it in its tracks before it does more harm. If you don't catch it in time, it may be necessary to perform some healing work to help those involved recover from any negative effects. In cases that the spell was working fine, but you changed your mind about what you wanted, it might take some time for things to get back to the way they were before you performed the working. Depending on what kind of spell you originally did, this could be a couple of days to a few weeks or months. Always be prepared to let time, patience, and healing work their magick when you've made a mistake that needs to be corrected.

Begin your spell-breaking ritual just as you would a normal closing ritual. Sit at your altar in front of the mirror box. Light you favorite incense, and take a moment to breathe and relax. When you feel ready, use the index finger of your subordinate hand to begin tracing a banishing pentagram or spiral three times over the lid of the box. As you trace it, say three times:

Unwind, retract,
Unbend, unmeld.
Break the enchantment
Of this magick spell.
Unspark, diffract,
Undo, unrhyme.
Uproot what I've planted.
Turn back the tide.

Use a bolline, pocket knife, or the tip of a pair of scissors to carefully break the seal around the lid of the mirror box. Place the open box back on the altar. In the same fashion as before, trace three more banishing pentagrams or spirals over the open box as you repeat three times:

Everything turns back
To what it was before.

The sacred balance
Is fully restored.
The innocent are healed.
Their hands are unbound.
This spell is broken.
The power unwound.
Peace is restored
Between all involved.
This spell's laid to rest
Once and for all.

Hold your hands over the box. Imagine it glowing with bright, white light as you repeat the first verse three more times:

Unwind, retract,
Unbend, unmeld.
Break the enchantment
Of this magick spell.
Unspark, diffract,
Undo, unrhyme.
Uproot what I've planted.
Turn back the tide.

Finish breaking the spell by cleansing and disposing of the box and its contents according to the rituals listed in the first part of this chapter. Watch things carefully for a couple of weeks to assess whether further action needs to be taken. If the spell has left behind some residual negative effects – even after breaking it – it may be necessary to perform a working to help heal and bring peace between those who are still feeling the effects. Just as you would keep notes of your successes, also keep notes of your failures so that you can foresee possible mistakes when you cast in the future.

Other Mirror Magick

Up to this point, I've covered a wide variety of ways that mirror boxes can be used in magick to solve everyday problems, and to make significant changes in the practitioner's life. Although it's definitely my favorite magickal tool, this final chapter steps outside the mirror box to demonstrate other ways that mirrors can be incorporated into your daily practice. The following applications will discuss mirrors as a portal to the subconscious mind and astral plane. Here, hidden senses can be tapped into to awaken psychic powers, invoke visions through divination, and perform dreamwork by helping the practitioner connect with the mind of another person.

The connection that they have with the astral realm and the psyche makes mirrors the perfect tool to enhance any spell or ritual. Using mirrors as altars helps solidify the idea in the practitioner's mind that the work they carry out on the physical plane is also being manifested in the realm of the collective unconscious, and that anything they imagine can be manifested in the physical world with enough effort. Working mirrors into other spells opens the gateway between the worlds so that those thoughts can truly become form on all planes of existence.

The next pages present other ways in which I've used different mirrors in my spellwork. These are just a few ideas in a realm of endless possibilities. After reading this chapter, think of other ways that you can use mirrors of different sizes, shapes, and colors in your own spells. Whether you use a mirror as the altar top, as the main tool to drive the spell, or simply prop one up in your sacred space to help connect yourself with the astral plane, you might find yourself incorporating mirrors into a great deal of your future workings.

Scrying with Mirrors

Scrying is an ancient divination technique in which the practitioner gazes into flames, a pool of water, or another reflective surface in hopes of seeing visions or symbols that will predict future events, or to access hidden information that can assist the seer or their querent. Where the visions come from depends entirely on the beliefs of the seer. Those who are highly spiritual claim that the information is being channeled through the divination tool by an outside force, or perhaps some entity in the spirit world. Others believe that the tool simply helps them clear their mind so that they can get in touch with their natural psychic abilities. Once they can access the extra senses hidden in their subconscious, the visions they wish to see are able to more easily present themselves to the seer's conscious mind.

There are many tools and mediums that can be used for scrying, but the crystal ball is probably the most recognizable of them all. Made famous by pop culture, most people think of a turbin-capped psychic staring into the ball, waving her pointy fingertips over it as she calls out to the spirit world for information. Many people see the crystal ball as a toy taken straight from the movies, but it's actually an ancient psychic and spiritual tool found in many cultures across the globe, and is by no means used exclusively in witchcraft. The Penn Museum still houses a perfectly formed, fifty-five pound crystal ball from Qing dynasty that once found its home in the palace of Beijing Empress Cixi. Feng shui uses crystal balls to inspire harmony and positive energy, and to promote healing. Then there are cultures that use the ball for scrying, or to gain information about the past, present, or possible future events.

Despite its popularity, the crystal ball is definitely not the only scrying tool available. Different gemstones and metals have also been employed to give seers a glimpse into the unknown. Smooth chunks of smoky quartz (which is a material commonly used to make crystal balls), amethyst, and clear quartz are all popular choices. Highly polished black obsidian, brass, and silver have been used since early times to make mirrors both for looking glasses and scrying. Obsidian mirrors are still a preferred choice of today's seers, as the black surface cancels out much of the light and background reflections, and also creates a depth in the glass that's easy for the practitioner to gaze into during divination sessions.

One drawback to these more traditional scrying mirrors is their high cost. Even a small (3-4 inch) obsidian mirror can easily run you anywhere from $30.00 to $60.00 online. Many people get around these high costs by making their own scrying mirror at home. This is easily achieved by removing the glass from a picture frame, and coating one side of it with black spray paint. The paint creates a solid backing for the glass that makes it work exactly like more expensive obsidian or metal mirrors, but only costs a few dollars and a little bit of spare time to make.

Any picture frame can be turned into a scrying mirror, which makes it fully customizable. Some people will only scry in round mirrors, while others prefer rectangular glass. Some like small mirrors that make them focus in one area. Others need a larger mirror that allows them to gaze into different areas. The practitioner can choose the frame, size, and shape that they prefer. Try to pick a frame that calls out to you, and one that you'll be comfortable with handling for the duration of your divination sessions. You'll be holding the mirror in your lap or propping it up on a table for most of your sessions, so try to choose a frame that won't be too cumbersome to handle.

To Make the Mirror

Supplies: A picture frame of your choice, black spray paint, sheets of newspaper.

Remove the glass from the picture frame, and carefully place it on several sheets of newspaper. Work outside on a warm day if possible, and wear a mask to avoid inhaling paint fumes. In steady sweeping motions, apply an even coat of spray paint to one side of the glass. Keep the coat thin to avoid runs in the paint. Allow the first coat to dry thoroughly, and then apply a second coat in the same manner. Once the second coat is completely dry, hold the glass up to the light to check for any thin areas in the paint. Apply a third coat if needed.

Take care not to let leaves, dirt, bugs, or other debris get into the paint. Mistakes will need to be lightly sanded out with fine grade sand paper, and then covered up with an extra coat of paint. Allow the final coat to dry overnight. Place the glass back into the frame with the painted side toward the back. Put the frame back together, and hold it up for inspection. Your picture frame should now be a black mirror that's ready to be cleansed and empowered for scrying.

Empowering Your Scrying Mirror

Empowering your mirror before use will charge it with your energies, and help you connect with it on a psychic level. I recommend making the Psychic Seer's Mirror Wash before charging the mirror, which is a potion that I use to cleanse the glass for added strength and mental connectedness. The potion and the empowering ritual will be done during the full moon, but the potion will take at least a week to infuse. Plan both the construction of your mirror and the making of the potion in advance so that everything is ready on time.

Psychic Seer's Mirror Wash

Ingredients: ½ cup vodka (or 80% rubbing alcohol), 1 teaspoon mugwort, 1 teaspoon lavender flowers, a small piece of amethyst.

Combine all ingredients in a clear jar. Hold your hands over the open mouth of the jar. Open your third eye chakra, and feel your body's energy pulsing there. Move that energy down your arms and into your hands. Let it spill out of your palms into the jar. Say eleven times:

I charge this magick fluid
With the power of my third eye.
Bring visions up from the darkness
Every time I sit to scry.

Seal the jar when you feel ready, and keep it in a dark closet or drawer for one week to give the ingredients time to infuse thoroughly into the alcohol. At the end of the week, and only at night, strain the liquid into a bottle with a spray cap (a travel sized empty hairspray bottle is ideal). Reserve the amethyst, and drop it back into the potion. Discard the spent herbs.

Store the bottle in a dark place, away from sunlight, until the night of the full moon. On this night, place the bottle outside in the moonlight for several hours. Bring it back inside before sunrise, and return it to its dark hiding place. Keep the potion there when not in use. Use it only for washing and anointing divination tools, or to dress candles. While it doesn't necessarily go bad, I do recommend discarding any unused portion after one year, and making a fresh batch. Do not ingest.

If you're empowering your mirror on the same night, bring the potion inside after it has had time to absorb the moonlight. Spray a light mist over the surface of the mirror, and wipe it clean with a dry cloth or paper towel as you say eleven times:

> *I cleanse this mirror*
> *Of all past energies.*
> *I wash away the old.*
> *I wipe the slate clean.*

Hold your hands over the mirror. Just as you did when you made the mirror wash, open your third eye chakra. Feel it pulsing with your energy. Send this energy down your arms, out of your palms, and into the mirror. Flood the mirror with your power while you say eleven times:

> *This mirror is now a portal*
> *That opens up between the worlds.*
> *It opens up my mind*
> *To every vision that unfolds.*
> *This glass is now the door,*

My mind is now the key.
Psychic visions, come to me.

When you feel ready, take the mirror outside. Let it sit in the moonlight for several hours. Bring it inside before sunrise, and keep it wrapped in a black cloth when not in use. Repeat this cleansing and empowering ritual during any full moon when you feel the mirror needs to be recharged.

Using the Black Mirror

Scrying doesn't come easily to everyone. It's an art that takes patience, practice, and an open mind. Many new scryers don't realize that it's normal not to see anything during the first few sessions. They get frustrated when images or visions fail to show up in the glass right away, and give up after just a few tries. Because everyone's brain works differently, each person will have a different experience, and will have to learn by trial and error how they best communicate with their scrying tool. People with more developed psychic abilities might see vivid images such as symbols, pictures, or even events playing out in the glass as if they were watching a recording. Others see only vague outlines, colored clouds, or the scrying medium itself will appear to change hues. Some claim that they don't see actual images in the medium, but that the trance they go into during scrying opens their mind to allow visions or symbols to come through mentally.

The most common way to scry with a black mirror is to sit in a dark room by the light of a single candle. Place the candle behind the mirror so that it's not reflected in the glass, but so that there's enough illumination to see into its depths. If you can, sit close enough to the mirror that you can see into it, but far enough away that your own reflection doesn't appear. You can also hold the mirror in your lap, and tilt it so that you can see into it, but aren't able to see your own reflection. Take a few deep breaths to clear your mind, and gaze passively into the depths of the glass. Stay relaxed and open-minded. Feel free to stare into different areas until you start to see changes taking place in the mirror.

At this point, what you see will depend entirely on your brain's psychic abilities, and the way that it communicates with you on that level.

As a warm up exercise, I like to ask the mirror to show me a few randomly chosen images, just to see how open my brain is during that session. I try to ask simple things like, "show me a star," or "show me an anchor," then wait for the images to produce themselves in the glass. I take each image one at a time to give my mind time to communicate with the mirror. If I'm having a good day, I can usually get at least outlines of the symbols to show up rather quickly. If I'm not feeling very connected at that moment, I won't see much of anything. Then I know that I need to come back at a later time.

When you first start practicing scrying, you might only see fuzzy shapes, dense clouds that change colors, or the glass will appear to change colors on its own. Some people really never advance farther than this, so don't be disheartened if you have trouble seeing things with picture perfect clarity. As you progress, you should be able to see clearer images. You might even get to the point that you can see images moving in the glass as if you were watching a security video or television show. Just remember that seeing images this clearly takes time and practice, and, again, comes more easily to some than it does to others.

As you get more comfortable with scrying, you can start asking the mirror to show you specific things. If you want to look in on someone who's far away, call out their name, and ask the mirror to show you how they're doing. If you want to see your life in the next twenty years, you could ask to see what kind of car you'll drive, the house you'll live in, who your spouse will be, et cetera. If you don't have a specific question in mind, simply let the mirror show you whatever images are coming through at that time. You might find that it ends up answering some questions you didn't even know you had.

Be sure to write down anything that you do see, and take time to interpret the symbols and images. Even different colored clouds could have something to tell you, so don't immediately write them off as a failed attempt. For example, red might mean a new romance, light green or gold might signify money on the way, black or dark, swampy green could warn of illness, et cetera. Look online or in divination books for common interpretations of your visions, or use your intuition to interpret the symbols yourself. I like to discuss the things I've seen with like-minded friends so that we can trade ideas about what some of the less obvious symbols might mean. It's also a good idea to pay close attention to your dreams after scrying, as your subconscious will likely still be trying to convey information after the session has ended.

Scrying Tips and Tricks

Many of the electronic devices that we have grown attached to can serve as scrying mirrors when one is either unavailable or impractical. Tablets, smartphones, and LCD television screens all make excellent candidates. I've done scrying sessions right in the middle of coffee shops by turning off my smartphone, and tilting the glass so that any distracting reflections were out of sight. The screen worked exactly like my mirror at home, and no one else in the room knew what I was doing. They simply thought that I was engrossed in whatever I was looking at on my phone.

While you can perform scrying any time, it's best to do so at night. You want the room to be completely dark so that only the displaced candlelight is illuminating the glass. You can also scry outside by the light of the moon, as long as you're away from unnatural light sources that will cause unwanted reflections. If you do scry during the day, be sure the room is completely dark except for the dim light of the candle flame. Keep all scrying tools wrapped in dark cloth — or stored away in a dark place — when not in use. Try not to expose your mirror to sunlight. Sunlight is said to wipe away its power, which means the mirror will have to be recharged under the full moon with the mirror wash.

Look into the depths of the glass rather than at the surface. This takes some practice, but will come naturally once you get the hang of it. If you have trouble with this at first, try placing the mirror on the floor near the corner of the room. The walls should be free of any pictures, decorations, doors, et cetera that will reflect in the glass. What you do want to see is the reflection of the corner where the walls and the ceiling come together. Sit close enough to the mirror that you can see into it, but far enough away that your own reflection is out of sight. As you relax into the session, let your eyes follow the line that the corner creates down into the depths of the glass. With practice, you'll be able to ignore the reflection of the corner, and can eventually drop the exercise altogether (although I do still use this trick on nights that I'm having trouble connecting during a session).

Stay as relaxed as possible. Take a few deep breaths before you begin, and try to completely clear your mind. If you have a preferred meditation or trance technique, feel free to begin each session in this way. Do whatever it takes to open your mind to the information that the mirror will be channeling. Stop the session if frustration sets in, or if you're not feeling a connection at that time.

Limit sessions to ten or fifteen minutes if you're new to scrying. The activity can be mentally exhausting at first, so it's crucial to gradually work your way up to longer sessions. Add a few minutes here and there as you become more comfortable, but still try to limit sessions to thirty or forty-five minutes. Stop if your eyes feel strained, if your head starts to hurt, or if your body feels uncomfortable after being in the same position for too long.

Casting Spells with the Black Mirror

One interesting experience that I've had with my scrying mirror is that I'll often see things in real life that I asked the mirror to show me during a recent session. The times that this has happened to me, the things I've seen were what I asked the mirror to show me during my warm up. Last fall, for example, I asked the mirror to show me a rabbit, a top hat, and an anchor. I was having trouble connecting with the mirror that night, so all I saw in the cloudy glass were outlines that never fully materialized. A few nights later, however, all three things that I asked to see showed themselves to me in real life.

It started with the rabbits. I had just gotten off work, and was driving to a coffee shop to get some writing done. I was driving down the winding road that leads downtown when I looked to my right. The hill on the side of the road was completely covered with brown rabbits. Despite the fact that it was a cold October night, and the sprinklers were on full blast, the rabbits sat completely still under the spraying water. Their heads moved in tandem as I drove by, each one of them seeming to watch me intently.

The event struck me as odd, but I didn't think much of it until I got to the coffee shop. As I was waiting in line to buy my drink, a tall woman in front of me bumped into me when she turned to leave the line. She was covered in exquisitely done tattoos. The first one to catch my attention was on her shoulder: a giant anchor on which a mermaid was provocatively perched. Then, when I sat down with my coffee drink, I noticed that two women at the next table both had anchors on their clothes. One was wearing a headband with small anchors on it, and the other was wearing a top that was completely covered in them.

The scrying session started coming back to me, but at that point I just thought it was an amusing coincidence. Then, about half an hour later, the cast of a touring musical walked through the door. They were all dressed in their elegant period costumes, right down to the top hats that the three men were sporting. One of them even dramatically tipped his hat at me as he walked by my table.

There have been other occasions in which the same thing has happened, even if I wasn't able to see the images while I was actually scrying. Seeing so many symbols in real life that I had recently asked to see during my sessions gave me the idea that the black mirror might be a useful tool for manifesting spells on the physical plane. The following spell is a template for anything you want to bring out of the mirror into the physical world. The process is simple and straightforward. Visualize your goal while sending your energy into the mirror, and ask that your specific want or need be shown to you in the physical realm. Change the chant to fit your specific purpose, and add whatever flair you want to the working. Take note of any images that appear during casting so that you can interpret them, and so that you know what to keep an eye out for should the symbols show themselves later.

Supplies: A candle of any color (or one of a color that matches your need), a black scrying mirror.

Sit in a dark room by the light of the candle. Sit on the floor with your scrying mirror flat in front of you. Ensure that the mirror doesn't show your own reflection, or that of other objects in the room.

Begin to gently rub your hands together until they feel warm and tingly. Hold them a few inches apart, and feel your body's magnetic energy pulsing in between your palms. Slowly let your palms drift farther apart as the energy grows between them. Concentrate on your goal for a few moments as the energy grows stronger.

When you feel ready, lower the energy ball into the mirror. Allow your palms to hover over the glass as you continue to pour your energy into it. Say eleven times:

> *I call out to the abyss.*
> *To the darkness,*
> *Void of light.*
> *Churn and breathe.*
> *Move and hiss.*
> *Bring my spell to life.*

At this point, recite a chant that you have written specific to your goal. Keep sending your energy into the glass as you repeat your original chant eleven times.

When you're finished, seal the spell by tracing a pentacle (or your favorite magickal symbol) over the glass three times. Each time you trace it, say:

> *Show me what I've asked to see.*
> *Make it happen.*
> *Make it be.*

If you choose, perform a scrying session to see what the mirror has to show regarding your spell. When you're finished, wrap the mirror in a dark cloth, and store it in a safe place away from sunlight.

Ray Baker

Nostradamus' Scrying Bowl

The famous prophet Nostradamus is known for using hydromancy, or scrying in the reflective surface of a pool of water, to summon the visions that eventually became his predictions. Some seers prefer hydromancy over catoptromancy (scrying in mirrors) because they believe that water is a natural psychic conduit that has the power to channel information to the seer. The elemental associations with water give hydromancy a more natural feel, and make it possible to perform in various ways such as indoors in a dark bowl, or outside at night by gazing into a fountain, birdbath, lake, or even a puddle of water.

The best scrying bowls are ones that are either already black, or that have been painted black. Like the black mirror, the dark finish helps cancel out unwanted light and reflections that can interfere with seeing visions in the water. Those who practice Wicca or another branch of European witchcraft might already have a cauldron on hand, which works perfectly as a scrying bowl. Other cast iron pots, black plastic bowls, or black clay pottery will serve the same purpose. If you're unable to get your hands on any of these options, find a clear glass or plastic bowl that you'll not use for food again. Coat the outside of the bowl with several layers of black spray paint, just as you would if you were making a scrying mirror. Once the paint is dry, keep the bowl in a dark place until you're ready to use it.

To use the bowl, fill it three-fourths of the way with clean water (I like to use collected rainwater that I've let sit for several hours in the light of the full moon, but regular tap water will work just fine). Sit in a dark room by the light of a single candle, making sure that the water is free of reflections. Add in eleven drops of the Psychic Seer's Mirror Wash. Hold your hands over the bowl. Open your third eye chakra, and imagine your power pulsing there. Send that energy down through your arms, out of your hands, and into the water. Concentrate on empowering the water as you say eleven times:

This bowl is now a portal
That opens up between the worlds.
It opens up my mind

To every vision that unfolds.
This water is now the door,
My mind is now the key.
Psychic visions, come to me.

From here, you'll scry in the pool of water just as you would in the black mirror. You do, however, have more options for incorporating correspondences by adding them to the water. Adding in the mirror wash is one way to work herbal correspondences into the spell. If you have certain herbs that you prefer to use, steep them in vodka or rubbing alcohol a few days in advance, then strain off the spent herbs. Add the liquid to the water to enhance its power. Small chunks of amethyst, smoky quartz, clear quartz, or obsidian can be dropped in as long as they don't distract you while you stare into the bowl. Your favorite essential oils can be dripped into the water as you ask your question or state your intention. You can then look for images that appear in the patterns that form as the oils spread out across the surface of the water.

When you finish your session, discard the water on the ground outside. Clean and dry the bowl before putting it away. Scrying bowls are less strict with being exposed to sunlight, because the water itself is the channel for the visions. The bowl is filled with fresh water and empowered before each session, so it's not absolutely necessary to keep the vessel out of the light. However, as part of taking good care of your magickal tools, bowls that are made specifically for scrying should still be wrapped in a dark cloth, and stored in a dark place. If you're using a cauldron, earthenware bowl, or other pot that will be used for other purposes, be sure to clean it thoroughly to remove any oils or herbs that shouldn't come in contact with food or drink.

Scrying Bowl Spell to Make Someone Dream of You

The scrying bowl, like the black mirror, can be used as a vessel in which to cast spells. Much like a cauldron, the ingredients are combined inside the bowl, and empowered by sending energy into the water, which represents the astral realm. One of my favorite scrying bowl spells was written to make someone dream of me. I had lost touch with an old friend that I really wanted to hear from. I no longer had her number in my phone, and she was off the grid online. I cast this spell so that I would show up in her dreams, and hopefully stay on her mind until she contacted me. Two days after casting the spell, I did indeed receive a text message from my friend. She'd been having weird dreams about me the last couple of nights, and wanted to share them with me to see if I could give her some insight as to what they meant.

This spell can easily be rewritten to give someone nightmares. I will admit that I did cast it at one point on someone who was about to renege on an important promise they'd made to me. In my case, I wrote the spell so that they would have nightmares about me until they made things right. It did work, but I experienced my own vivid nightmares for the few nights that the spell was active. How you use it is entirely up to you. Just remember that performing this working for the sole purpose of harassing someone will have negative effects on you. Be prepared for the repercussions if you choose to use this working for darker purposes.

You can perform this working at any time, but it's best to do it at night, or when you know your target will be sleeping.

Supplies: A purple candle, a black scrying bowl filled with clean water (collected rain water if possible), three of your favorite essential oils (I prefer Dragon's Blood, Cool Water, and Neroli for this working), your favorite incense, a photo of the target (or their name written on a slip of paper).

Light the candle and incense. Turn off any other lights so that the room is only illuminated by the candle.

Write your target's name nine times on the back of the photo, or on the slip of paper. Call out their name three times each time you write it. Make the letters thick and dark, and see that person clearly in your mind as you work. Place the photo or paper in the center of the altar, and set the scrying bowl directly on top of it.

Take several deep breaths, and let yourself fall into a trance. Stare into the darkness of the water as you concentrate on the target of the spell. Slowly add three drops of each essential oil to the water, and whisper the person's name on each drop.

Begin rubbing your hands together until they feel warm and tingly. Bring them a few inches apart, and feel the energy pulsing between your palms. Let the energy build for a few moments. Feel it pulsing and growing, and pushing your hands slowly apart. Imagine that the energy is a bright ball of purple light hovering between your palms.

Whisper into the energy ball three times the name of the target. See their face clearly in your mind as you lower the ball of energy into the water. Let your palms hover over the surface of the water while you continue pouring your energy into it. Imagine that the bowl is the open skull of your target, and that the water is a portal into their imagination. Say nine times:

(person's name),
Hear my words as clearly
As if they were your own.
I am inside your head.
You are not alone.

Now visualize yourself sitting behind the person while they sleep soundly in their bed. Keep pushing your energy into the water as you see yourself massaging their scalp with the tips of your fingers. Repeat at least nine times:

(person's name),
I call out to your subconscious mind.
I dig my fingers deep inside
The recesses of your thoughts and dreams.
Your subconscious mind cannot ignore me.
Turn your attention on the words I say.
Hear them as clearly as the light of day.
Bend your mind's ear, and let your thoughts ignite
With visions of me as you sleep at night.

Return to your visualization of the bowl as your target's open skull. Let your hands rest now on your legs or at your sides. Gaze into the water, knowing that as you do, you're gazing into your target's mind. Visualize exactly what you want the person to dream about, and send these thoughts into the water. Try to see your visualization playing out in the depths of the bowl, and hold it in your mind for as long as you can.

When you feel ready, trace a pentacle (or your favorite magickal symbol) over the bowl three times. Each time you trace it, say:

> *Show (person's name)*
> *What I've asked them to see.*
> *Make it happen.*
> *Make it be.*

Cover the bowl tightly with a black cloth, or rest a black piece of construction paper over the top. Leave the bowl on the altar, and repeat the spell each night until you hear from the person that you're attempting to contact, or until you wish to end the spell. When you're ready to close the working, discard the water on the ground outside, and clean the bowl thoroughly with soap and water.

Mirrors as Altars

Part of the fascination that humans have with mirrors is the parallel universe that seems to open up on the other side of the glass. The flat surface becomes a world exactly like our own, but flipped backwards on itself. The border between the worlds is so thin that you could almost reach right through the glass, and fall headfirst into the alternate universe on the other side. Lewis Carroll had the same idea when he let Alice step through the mirror in *Through the Looking-Glass*. The mirror served as the doorway to a realm that Alice had visited before in her dreams. One in which strange entities do strange things, and everything is the opposite of what it should be.

Many people with alternative beliefs are familiar with the concept that Carroll touched on in his stories. Known as the astral plane, this is the realm of our imaginations. This is where dreams come to life, and thoughts take form. It's where we go while in deep meditation, or when our consciousness travels outside of our bodies during sleep. I think of it as a construction of our collective consciousness; an entire universe that has been built by all of our interconnected thoughts, dreams, and even nightmares. It's a very real part of our existence that we can only access with the power of the mind.

As an extension of our minds, the astral realm is where all of our needs and desires first take form. Unlike Alice, we can't physically travel to this other dimension (at least not yet). However, humans do have the amazing ability to physically manifest their visions from that plane by focusing their energy and intent on an idea until it becomes reality. Every manmade object was once just an idea that came out of a want or need in someone's mind. The ability of humans to connect the physical world with the dimension of the mind has made our world rich with electric lights, skyscrapers, airplanes, computers, music, and the vast array of other objects and technology that no other animal on Earth has yet to create.

The same concept applies to magick. A woodworker sees a chair in his mind, and then focuses his talent, skill, and creative energy to bring that chair into physical existence out of raw materials. A witch sees someone who's sick, and then focuses their energy and intent into making that person well using a spell, potion, or other technique that they've mastered over time. In both cases, a need is visualized in the mind, and energy focused on that need until it becomes part of the physical reality.

Practitioners of many paths know this theory by the saying "as above, so below", which is said by many followers to be the key to all magick. This esoteric phrase is actually a shortened segment taken from an ancient document known as "The Emerald Tablet of Hermes". This short working has ancient Egyptian roots, and was believed by followers of Hermeticism to have been carved into emerald by Hermes Trismegistus himself. The original tablets have never been found. However, translations of the content have been uncovered in many languages and religious texts dating as far back as c.800.

The original text, as taken from a translation featured in *The Emerald Tablet of Hermes*, reads:

> This is true, and far distant from a lie; whatever is below, is like that which is above; and that which is above, is like that which is below: By this are acquired and perfected the miracles of the One Thing (9).

While the origins of "The Emerald Tablet" are still embedded in myth and legend, it has nevertheless kept alchemists, magicians, and scholars in awe for ages. It was the keystone of Egyptian magick and alchemy. As part of Hermetic teachings, the phrase "as above, so below" also made its way into Freemasonry. Aleister Crowley, whose beliefs were heavily influenced by both Egyptian religion and Freemasonry, was greatly responsible for turning the saying into a central teaching of modern day Wicca. Even the Bible hints at the idea in the Lord's Prayer when it says, "let your will be done, on Earth as it is in Heaven" (*New Heart English Bible,* Mat. 6.10).

Using mirrors as altars, or in conjunction with altars, brings the key phrase "as above, so below" directly into daily practice, and unlocks the door between the worlds of the physical body and the mind. Mirrors remind us that what we do on the physical plane is also taking form in our minds, and that anything we imagine can be manifested in the physical world with enough effort. When I see my altar in the mirror, I know that the actions I'm performing on the physical plane are also taking place in the astral realm. As the candles burn down on the altar, so, too, do they burn down in the dimension of my mind. When I raise my cone of power in my circle, I know that those energies are also being raised on the astral plane.

For these reasons, mirrors have become a central part of my personal altar and sacred space. Many times, I place a large mirror directly over my altar, and set up my materials on the glass. Other times, I hang a mirror behind my altar so that I can see my working being acted out in the astral plane as I perform the appropriate actions in the physical realm. Doing so opens my mind, and connects the two worlds within my sacred space. The following ritual is one example of a working that I always perform over a large mirror, and shows how they can be used to enhance nearly any kind of spellwork.

The Love Altar

The Love Altar is a ritual that I've done several times over the years. It's designed to make more room in your life for love by reminding yourself that you deserve to be loved, and by opening your heart to love so that it can flow freely into your life. It also helps heal from past traumas such as break-ups, abuse, or other bad past relationships so that you have the courage to move forward and try again. Since the ritual works to bring love into all areas of your life (the mind, body, and soul), it uses a mirror as the altar to represent love being manifested on all planes.

This working can function as both a healing ritual, and a spell to bring new romantic interests into your life. My experience with the spell is that it will bring several options out of the woodwork. It might help you meet new people that you could potentially date, or it might come to your attention that someone you already know has had a thing for you for quite some time. Although several options might present themselves after you set up your love altar, remember that you don't have to latch on to the first thing that comes along. Some of the people who have shown up after I've done this working were good choices. Others, not so much. I strongly encourage going on several dates with any potential love interests, and taking time to get to know them before you make any definite decisions. Never sell yourself short to the first person who shows interest in you, and never immediately get into a relationship with someone until you know they're a good choice. Enjoy the results of the ritual, but always use the same caution and intelligence that you would want to use in any other dating situation.

It should be noted that this ritual isn't just for those who are looking for a new romantic relationship. Love means many different things to different people. When you cast this spell to bring more love into your life, it could come in the form of new friends, a new pet, creating stronger bonds with existing friends and family members, or even learning to have more love and respect for yourself. For some, this might be just the spell they need to remind themselves that they're beautiful, and deserve all the love that the universe has to give. When you need to bring more love into your life, whether it's a new partner, new friends, or learning to love yourself, set up this altar, and let the energy of love flow freely into your life.

I've always started this ritual on the new moon, and kept the candles burning until the full moon. At that point, I let the candles burn out, and see how things are going while the moon is waning. I'll light fresh candles at the next new moon if I want to keep the loving and healing energies flowing, or if I want to continue weighing my romantic options. Like any spell, the moon can be used in different ways depending on your needs. If you want to banish hatred or loneliness, or the pain of a relationship gone wrong, rework the spell to be done during the waning moon. Other purposes such as helping love grow, healing from past hurts, or making new connections should be done between the new and full moon.

For this working, you'll need to make a love oil, or have one prepared that you already prefer. The following is the recipe that I always use when I perform this ritual. This oil has heat to it, but is also sweet and sensual, and reminds me of love intertwined with passion and sexuality. Make this oil if you have access to the essential oils that it requires, or use any oil that represents love to you. You can also change the attributes that are listed to better match your specific goal, or what you're looking for in a partner.

Supplies: A clean glass vial or bottle, a red or pink candle, your favorite incense, seven clean plastic eyedroppers, a fine-tipped permanent marker, the following essential oils: lemon, orange blossom, passion fruit, cool water, cinnamon, lavender, and dragon's blood (Sun's Eye brand smells the best, and you can easily find it online).

Light the candle and incense in the name of love. Take several deep breaths, and enjoy the scent of the smoke as you let yourself fall into a state of deep relaxation. As you relax, slowly chant in sets of three:

I raise love here in this hour.
I raise love for myself.
I raise love for others.
I raise the ability

Inside the Mirror Box

To be loved by others.
I am love,
And I am loved.

With a clean eyedropper (use a clean one for each oil), add seven drops of lemon oil to your vial. As you do so, say three times:

I invoke truth
Upon this potion.
Bring me a lover
Who speaks only the truth.

Add in seven drops of orange blossom oil while you say three times:

I invoke fidelity
Upon this potion.
Keep my lover faithful
To me, and only me.

Add in seven drops of passion fruit oil while you say three times:

I invoke passion
Upon this potion.
Bring me a lover
With passion in his/her heart.

Add in three drops of cinnamon oil while you say three times:

I invoke sexual power
Upon this potion.
Let things stay steamy
Between the sheets.

Add in two drops of lavender oil as you say three times:

Ray Baker

I invoke romance
Upon this potion.
Bring me a lover
Who does all the right things.

Add three drops of cool water oil as you say three times:

I invoke serenity
Upon this potion.
Bring me a lover
With a cool head and tender heart.

Add three drops of dragon's blood oil as you say three times:

I invoke protection
Upon this potion.
Keep me safe on my journey
To find the love I deserve.

Cap the vial, and begin slowly rolling it back and forth between your palms. Let the energy in your hands pour into the oil, and repeat three times:

I charge this potion
With the energy of love.
It is now a magnet
Which love and passion
Find irresistible.
Love and passion
Seek out this oil,
And bless anything
And everything it touches.

Draw a heart on the vial with the permanent marker, and keep it in a cool, dark place until ready to use.

Inside the Mirror Box

When it comes time to set up the Love Altar, perform the ritual as follows:

Supplies: A mirror large enough to cover the table that you're designating as your altar (or a table with a mirror built into the top), love oil, four white Catholic-style jar candles, four red Catholic-style jar candles, white and red glitter, a large chunk each of rose quartz and clear quartz, 11 small gemstones of your choice, the Ace of Hearts from a deck of playing cards, the Ace of Cups and Temperance cards from a Tarot deck (you can print them off of the internet to avoid damaging the cards from your personal deck. A strip of paper folded into a right-angled triangle and glued to the back of each image will make it stand on its own), a favorite picture of yourself, a representation of each element (I use lava stones for Fire, water dyed with dragon's blood ink for Water, salt for Earth, and Nag Champa incense for Air), a copy of the key to your home.

Begin by placing your mirror face-up on the altar. Wave your dominant hand over the mirror as if you were wiping it clean, but without touching the glass. As you concentrate on sending your energy into the mirror, say three times:

I cleanse this mirror
Of all the energies
That it may have gathered
Along its path to me.

Hold both of your hands over the mirror. Continue to charge it with your energy as you say three times:

I consecrate this mirror
In the powerful name of love.
Let love reflect back up
As it shines down from above.
Energy of love,
Hear my plea.
Energy of love,
Come quickly to me.

Let there be love.
Let there be love.
Let there be love.

Turn to the north. Hold up the object that you have chosen to represent the element of Earth. Say:

Element of Earth,
Keeper of the watchtower of the north,
I call on thee.
I invite you into this sacred space
To aid me in this working.
I invite you into this sacred space
To witness this magickal rite.
Bring love into this temple.
Make love grow here tonight.

Turn to the east. Hold up the object that you have chosen to represent the element of Air. Say:

Element of Air,
Keeper of the watchtower of the east,
I call on thee.
I invite you into this sacred space
To aid me in this working.
I invite you into this sacred space
To witness this magickal rite.
Bring love into this temple.
Make love grow here tonight.

Turn to the south. Hold up the object that you have chosen to represent the element of Fire. Say:

Element of Fire,
Keeper of the watchtower of the South,

I call on thee.
I invite you into this sacred space
To aid me in this working.
I invite you into this sacred space
To witness this magickal rite.
Bring love into this temple.
Make love grow here tonight.

Turn to the West. Hold up the object that you have chosen to represent the element of Water. Say:

Element of Water,
Keeper of the watchtower of the west,
I call on thee.
I invite you into this sacred space
To aid me in this working.
I invite you into this sacred space
To witness this magickal rite.
Bring love into this temple.
Make love grow here tonight.

Stand in the center of the circle. Hold your hands over your head, with your palms opened up toward the ceiling. Say:

Great feminine creative energy
Of the universe,
Keeper of the darkness of night,
The bright moon high in the sky,
The yin to the yang,
The darkness that overpowers
The light of day,
I invite you into this sacred space
To aid me in this working.
I invite you into this sacred space
To witness this magickal rite.

Bring love into this temple.
Make love grow here tonight.

Move your hands down so that they're parallel to your hips, and your palms are opened up toward the ground. Say:

Great masculine creative energy
Of the universe,
Keeper of the brightest days,
The burning sun high in the sky,
The yang to the yin,
The bright morning light
That conquers the dark of night,
I invite you into this sacred space
To aid me in this working.
I invite you into this sacred space
To witness this magickal rite.
Bring love into this temple.
Make love grow here tonight.

Stand at the altar. Take three deep breaths, and clear your mind. Say:

I stand before this altar,
In this place between the worlds.
I open myself to love.
I open my mind, my heart, and my soul.
I open myself to love for others.
I open myself to love for myself.
I open myself to love from others.
Fill me with love, above all else.

Take a moment to feel your energy rising up inside you, and filling every cell in your body. Imagine yourself glowing with a warm, soft red light, and know that you're filled with the sacred energy known as love.

When you feel ready, flip over the photo of yourself, and write on the back:

I am always reminded
That I am beautiful,
Smart, and that I deserve love.
Fill my life with people
Who will see me for who I am,
Love me for who I am,
And who deserve the love
I have to give.

Prop the photo up on the altar away from the candles. Repeat the chant 11 times while charging the photo with your energy, and imagining yourself glowing with a bright, white light.

Turn over the printed image of the Temperance card, and write on the back:

I keep one foot planted
Firmly on the ground,
But let one dangle in the water
Where love can flow freely.
Let me remain patient,
Yet persistent, as love takes
The time it needs to grow.

Prop the image up on the altar away from the candles. Fill it with your energy as you repeat the chant 11 times.

Turn over the image of the Ace of Cups, and write on the back:

My cup runneth over with love.
Love for myself,
Love for others,
And the ability

To be loved by others.
Love flows freely
Into my life.

Prop the image up on the altar, away from the candles. Send your energy into it as you repeat the verse 11 more times.

If you're performing this working with the intention of finding a new lover, take the Ace of Hearts playing card in your hands. Hold it between your palms, and charge it with your energy as you say 11 times:

I call out to my
Ace of Hearts.
That one person
Who is right for me.
Hear my voice
Inside your mind,
And follow it back to me.

Prop the card up on the altar against the bowl of water, or another object on the altar that will not be near the candles.

Pick up the white jar candle. Anoint it with love oil, working from the middle towards each end until you have gone all the way around the candle. As you work around the candle, say three times:

I charge this candle
With healing power.
All past hurts and traumas
Melt away under its flame.
Turn my insecurities to ash.
Burn away all of my fears.
Heal my heart of the past.
Let love reappear.

Dry your fingertips on the trimmed wick so that it also gets anointed. Place the candle in the center of the altar, and light it. Hold your hands around the candle, and charge it as you repeat the chant three more times.

Pick up the red jar candle, and begin anointing it in the same fashion. As you do so, say three times:

I charge this candle
With love and passion.
Love and lust rise up
In its burning flame.
This light is a beacon.
It serves as the guide
To lead love and passion
Into my life.

Dry your fingertips on the trimmed wick. Place the candle on the altar, about three inches from the white one, and light it. Charge it with your energy, in the same manner as the white one, while you repeat the chant three more times.

Hold the chunk of rose quartz in your hands. Roll it around in your palms, and imagine it glowing with a soft, pink light as you fill it with your energy. Say three times:

I raise love inside this circle.
I raise passion inside this circle.
I raise love for myself inside this circle.
I raise love for others inside this circle.
I raise the ability to be loved
By others inside this circle.

Love, fill my heart.
Love, fill my mind.
Love, fill my soul.
Love, I invite you into my life.

Place the rose quartz wherever you want on the altar. Repeat this process with the clear quartz.

Pick up the eleven small gemstones. Shake them gently in your closed hands. Fill them with your energy, and imagine them glowing with the same soft, pink light while you repeat the verse three more times. Place the stones, one at a time, all over the altar. Say each time:

I deserve love,
And it will be mine.

Anoint the key to your home with one drop of love oil while you say three times:

This, the key to my home,
Is also the key to my loyal heart.
I whisper to that special someone,
The one who's meant just for me.
Let him/her follow the power of this spell.
Bring him/her swiftly to claim this key.

Put the key on the altar between the two burning candles. Next, slowly sprinkle the white glitter all over the altar while you say three times:

I charge this altar
With healing power.
All past hurts and traumas
Melt away upon its surface.
Turn my insecurities to ash.
Burn away all of my fears.
Heal my heart of the past.
Let love reappear.

Repeat this process with the red glitter as you say three times:

I charge this altar
With love and passion.
Love and lust rise up
From its mirrored surface.
This light is a beacon.
It serves as the guide
To lead love and passion
Into my life.

Relax for a moment, and imagine your entire space filling with warm, loving energy. Let it well up from inside you, and spill out of your body into your surroundings. Feel the energy growing stronger and stronger as you repeat 11 times:

I sit before this altar,
In this place between the worlds.
I open myself to love.
I open my mind, my heart, and my soul.
I open myself to love for others.
I open myself to love for myself.
I open myself to love from others.
Fill me with love, above all else.

Repeat this in sets of 11 as many times as you like. Each time you say it, let the loving energy that you're raising get stronger and warmer.

When you feel ready, stand, and turn to the west. Say:

Element of Water,
Keeper of the watchtower of the west,
I thank you
For aiding me in this working.
I thank you
For witnessing this magickal rite.
Keep love in this temple.
Let it grow stronger each night.

Bow respectfully to the west, then turn to the south. Say:

Element of Fire,
Keeper of the watchtower of the south,
I thank you
For aiding me in this working.
I thank you
For witnessing this magickal rite.
Keep love in this temple.
Let it grow stronger each night.

Bow respectfully to the south, then turn to the east. Say:

Element of Air,
Keeper of the watchtower of the east,
I thank you
For aiding me in this working.
I thank you
For witnessing this magickal rite.
Keep love in this temple.
Let it grow stronger each night.

Bow respectfully to the east, then turn to the north. Say:

Element of Earth,
Keeper of the watchtower of the north,
I thank you
For aiding me in this working.
I thank you
For witnessing this magickal rite.
Keep love in this temple.
Let it grow stronger each night.

Move your hands down so that they're parallel to your hips, and your palms are opened up toward the ground. Say:

Great masculine creative energy
Of the universe,
Keeper of the brightest days,
The burning sun high in the sky,
The yang to the yin,
The bright morning light
That conquers the dark of night,
I thank you
For entering this sacred space
To aid me in this working.
I thank you
For witnessing this magickal rite.
Keep love in this temple.
Let it grow stronger each night.

Raise your hands over your head, with your palms opened up toward the ceiling. Say:

Great feminine creative energy
Of the universe,
Keeper of the darkness of night,
The bright moon high in the sky,
The yin to the yang,
The darkness that overpowers
The light of day,
I thank you
For entering this sacred space
To aid me in this working.
I thank you
For witnessing this magickal rite.
Keep love in this temple.
Let it grow stronger each night.

Kneel down, and rest your open palms on the floor. Feel yourself connecting with the earth, and let it ground the energies that are pulsing and vibrating inside you. Once you feel grounded, open the circle if you have cast one.

Keep a close eye on the candles. Use a fresh incense stick to transfer the flame to a new candle whenever one gets low (about ¼ inch of wax remaining). Allow any used candles to burn themselves out, and then remove them from the altar. Look for symbols in the spent wax to let you know how the spell is going.

Try to keep the candles burning until the full or new moon (depending on what you're using the ritual for), and then let them burn themselves out. Repeat the ritual as necessary.

Locker Mirror Protection Spell

When I was a teenager, there was a house in my neighborhood that I knew belonged to witches. I would pass the house each day as I walked to and from my job at the restaurant around the corner. As I walked by, I would admire the mirrors that were propped up in all the windows. Each one either had a silver frame with a colorful interwoven pentagram painted in the center, or was actually in the shape of a star. I loved seeing the mirrors, not only because the pentagram is my favorite shape, but also because I knew the secret meaning behind them.

Using mirrors in this way is another common folk spell that has been passed down through the ages in many spell books, as well as by word of mouth from one generation to the next. Like outward-facing mirror boxes, mirrors hung in windows or on the outsides of doors are said to create a protective barrier that repels negative energies and entities. Some practitioners believe that the mirrors force evil to stare itself in the face, thereby frightening it away from the property.

The best mirrors to use for this project are usually sold as locker or shower mirrors. However, any small, lightweight mirrors will work. Picture frames with glass that has been painted blue or black (in the same manner as a scrying mirror) will work great for this spell, too. The size and shape that you use is completely up to you. The mirrors may be left blank, or, like my neighbors did with theirs, you can paint protective symbols in the centers of the glass.

This spell will require some planning, so give yourself enough time before the full moon to find or make all the mirrors you'll need. Do you want one in each window, or one on every outside door? Do you want one on every inside door, too? Should you take one to work to hang outside your office, or prop up on your desk? Do you need to hang one on the shed door to protect your tools? Write down where you want to place each mirror so you don't forget. If you plan on painting any of them, do so in advance so that they're ready to charge on the night of the full moon.

While you wait for the full moon, you might also want to make a mirror wash that will cleanse and consecrate the mirrors in the name of protection. This wash is similar to the Psychic Seer's Wash, but uses common protection and warding herbs to charge the potion with those energies.

Mirror Wash for Protection

Ingredients: ½ cup vodka (or 80% rubbing alcohol), 1 teaspoon basil, 1 teaspoon sage, 1 pinch High John the Conqueror root, a small piece of hematite.

Combine all ingredients in a clear jar. Hold your hands over the open mouth of the jar, and pour your energy into it while you say nine times:

I charge this magick fluid
In the powerful name of protection.
Everything it touches will transform
Into a powerful, protective talisman.

Seal the jar when you feel ready, and keep it in a dark closet or drawer for one week to give the ingredients time to infuse thoroughly into the alcohol. At the end of the week, and only at night, strain the liquid into a bottle with a spray cap (a travel sized empty hairspray bottle is ideal). Reserve the hematite, and drop it back into the potion. Discard the spent herbs.

Store the bottle in a dark place, away from sunlight, until the night of the full moon. On this night, place the bottle outside in the moonlight for several hours. Bring it back inside before sunrise, and return it to its dark hiding place. Keep the potion there when not in use. Like the other mirror wash, use this potion only for washing and anointing magickal tools, or to dress candles. Discard any unused portion after one year, and make a fresh batch. Do not ingest.

Charging the Mirrors for Protection

During the full moon, take your mirrors and the potion outside. (If you don't have time to charge the potion and the mirrors on the same night, then try to make the potion in advance so that it's ready when the time comes to charge the mirrors.) One at a time, spray a light mist over the surface of each mirror, and wipe it clean with a dry cloth or paper towel as you say nine times:

I cleanse this mirror
Of all past energies.
I wash away the old.
I wipe the slate clean.

Hold your hands over the mirror. Concentrate on sending your energy into the glass as you say nine times:

I consecrate this mirror
In the name of protection.
All evil will flee from the light
That the mirror reflects back.
It is a wall, strong and bright,
That no danger can sneak past.

Place the mirror face-up on the ground in front of you. Repeat this process with each mirror. When you're finished, allow them to soak up the moonlight for several hours. Bring them back in before sunrise, and spend the next day hanging or propping them up where you've decided you need them. Recharge the mirrors every six months during the full moon.

Conclusion

As this journey through the dimension of the mirror box comes to an end, I breathe a heavy sigh of relief knowing that we made it out together. My journey definitely had its more difficult moments, but I can say that I came away from it a stronger and more mature person than I was before. I also came out of it a much stronger witch than I was before, as I had to develop my craft on various levels in order to deal with the people and situations that I encountered along my path.

It's my hope that you, as the reader, will also be able to use the information in this book to advance your own craft. No matter what path you're walking, I want you to be able to apply the spells and theories in the previous pages to your daily practice, and use them to become a stronger and more adept practitioner. I hope that you've learned something from this book that you haven't been able to find in the mass of witchcraft 101 books that flood the shelves of major bookstores. Something that will take your practice to the next level, and allow you to grow in multiple ways.

Most importantly, I want you to walk away from this book with increased confidence in yourself and your abilities, and with the knowledge needed to defend yourself in the face of adversity. I feel that the strongest message my work carries is that you don't have to lie down and take it when people treat you poorly, take advantage of you, or try to take what's rightfully yours. Playing nice simply won't be an option in some situations. You have an immense amount of power at your disposal that can, and should, be used to defend yourself on every level when the time is right to do so. Don't be afraid to stand up and fight for yourself.

Probably my biggest hope for this book is that my fellow practitioners will be able to further expand on the spells and information that I've provided. I'm confident that my book will serve as the foundation that mirror box magick continues to grow on from this point forward. Just as I was able to develop the two spells that I first learned into an entire system of magick, I want to see how far other witches can take what I've given them here. I want to see what other spells are inspired by the ones I've written. I want to see new and even more creative ways that other witches use the mirror box to solve problems that I haven't thought of yet.

I hope to hear back from my readers about their experiences with the box, and how it was able to bring amazing changes into their lives, just as it's done for me for more than ten years now. I can be found on Facebook at https://www.facebook.com/raybakerauthor. My Twitter account can be found at https://twitter.com/Ray_Baker_1111. Please keep me posted on how the mirror box works for you, what you thought of this book, and other ways that you've used the box in your personal practice.

Thank you for reading, and best of luck on your journey, wherever it takes you!

Happy Casting,

Ray Baker

Bibliography and Works Cited

Brinkmann, Ron. "Mirror Box." *Digital Composting*. 1 Dec. 2011. < https://
digitalcomposting.wordpress.com/2011/12/01/mirror-box/>

Brown, Michael Forbes. "The Dark Side of the Shaman." *Natural History
Magazine*. Nov. 1989: 8-10.

Carroll, Lewis. *Through the Looking-Glass*. New York: Barnes & Noble
Books, 2004.

Chesnut, Andrew R. *Devoted to Death: Santa Muerte, the Skeleton Saint*.
New York: Oxford University Press, 2012.

Frazer, James George. *The New Golden Bough*. New York: Criterion Books,
1959.

Graves, Julia. *The Language of Plants: A Guide to the Doctrine of Signatures*.
Great Barrington, MA: Lindisfarne Books, 2012.

Kail, Tony. *Santa Muerte: Mexico's Mysterious Saint of Death*. USA: Fringe
Research Press, 2010.

Mage, Abramelin the. *The Sacred Magic of Abramelin the Mage*. Ed. S.L.
MacGregor Mathers. Adobe Acrobat Edition. Adobe, 1998. < http://
hermetic.com/crowley/aa/abramelin1.pdf>

Moeller, W.O. *The Mithraic Origin and Meanings of the Rotas-Sator Square*.

Leiden, Netherlands: Brill Academic Publishing, 1997.

New Heart English Bible. Ed. Wayne A. Mitchell. Bloomington, IN:

AuthorHouse, 2009. Print.

Storms, Godfrid. *Anglo Saxon Magic*. Leiden, Netherlands: Martinus Nijoff

Publishers, 1948.

Trismegistus, Hermes. *The Emerald Tablet of Hermes*. IAP, 2009.

Updike, John. *The Witches of Eastwick*. New York: Alfred A. Knopf, 1984.

Index

Made in United States
North Haven, CT
29 September 2022